African Families in the Twenty-First Century

Short selected list of publications of Aderanti Adepoju

Population and Sustainable Development in Africa in the 21st Century: Challenges and Prospects. HRDC African Research Series No. 1. Lagos: Concept Publications, 2001.

Population, Poverty, Structural Adjustment Programmes and Quality of Life in Sub Saharan Africa. Research Paper No. 1 Dakar: PHRDA, IDEP, 1996.

Gender, Work and Population in Sub-Saharan Africa (edited with C. Oppong). London: ILO, Heinemann and James Currey, 1994.

The Impact of Structural Adjustment on the Population of Africa: The Implications for Education, Health and Employment (ed.). London: UNFPA, Heinemann and James Currey, 1993.

Family, Population and Development in Africa (ed.). London and New Jersey: Zed Books Ltd., 1997 (published in French as Politiques Demographiques et Developpement. Edition Karthala, Paris, 1999)

Adepoju, A. Dynamics of Ageing and Support of the Elderly in Nigeria. *HRDC Policy Paper No 2*. Lagos: Concept Publications, 2003a.

Adepoju, A. Feminization of poverty: perspectives from women in Nigeria's urban centres. *HRDC Research Series No. 4*. Lagos: Concept Publications, 2003b.

Note: Many of Prof Adepoju's publications have been translated into French and are in very wide circulation.

African Families in the Twenty-First Century

✦

Prospects and Challenges

Aderanti Adepoju

iUniverse, Inc.
New York Lincoln Shanghai

African Families in the Twenty-First Century
Prospects and Challenges

iUniverse books may be ordered through booksellers or by contacting:

iUniverse
2021 Pine Lake Road, Suite 100
Lincoln, NE 68512
www.iuniverse.com
1-800-Authors (1-800-288-4677)

Unless indicated as *Adepoju, Adunola*, all citings of *Adepoju* in this text refer to the author (given in the References as *Adepoju, Aderanti.*).

ISBN-13: 978-0-595-36464-0 (pbk)
ISBN-13: 978-0-595-80896-0 (ebk)
ISBN-10: 0-595-36464-0 (pbk)
ISBN-10: 0-595-80896-4 (ebk)

Printed in the United States of America

African Families in the Twenty-First Century

◆

Prospects and Challenges

Aderanti Adepoju

iUniverse, Inc.

New York Lincoln Shanghai

African Families in the Twenty-First Century
Prospects and Challenges

iUniverse books may be ordered through booksellers or by contacting:

iUniverse
2021 Pine Lake Road, Suite 100
Lincoln, NE 68512
www.iuniverse.com
1-800-Authors (1-800-288-4677)

Unless indicated as *Adepoju, Adunola*, all citings of *Adepoju* in this text refer to the author (given in the References as *Adepoju, Aderanti*.).

ISBN-13: 978-0-595-36464-0 (pbk)
ISBN-13: 978-0-595-80896-0 (ebk)
ISBN-10: 0-595-36464-0 (pbk)
ISBN-10: 0-595-80896-4 (ebk)

Printed in the United States of America

Contents

Background and Acknowledgements

A decade ago, the author coordinated the publication of a volume on Family, Population and Development in Africa, based on contributions from several specialists. This was our modest contribution to the International Year of the Family 1994. At that time, the United Nations stressed that the family was the basic unit of society, and one of its most enduring institutions.

Ten years on, the challenges facing African families have magnified due to a series of economic, social, political, ecological and other related factors. Some of these, as well as the opportunities facing African families in the new millennium, are explored in this volume.

Publication of the volume is made possible through the financial and technical support of the Human Resources Development Centre (HRDC), Lagos, Nigeria, and the skilful editorial services of Ms Biddy Greene. The views expressed in the text are those of the author and in no way reflect those of the HRDC.

Aderanti Adepoju
Lagos, Nigeria

Abbreviations and acronyms

AIDS	Acquired Immune Deficiency Syndrome
DHS	Demographic and Health Survey
DRC	Democratic Republic of Congo
FGC	Female genital cutting
FWCW	Fourth World Conference on Women
HIV	Human Immunodeficiency Virus
HRDC	Human Resources Development Centre (Lagos)
ICPD	International Conference on Population and Development
IDEP	African Institute for Economic Development and Planning
ILO	International Labour Organization
IYF	International Year of the Family
IPPF	International Planned Parenthood Federation
LRA	Lord's Resistance Army
MOST	Management of Social Transformation
OAU	Organization of African Unity
PHRDA	Population and Human Resources Development in Africa
RENAMO	Resistência Nacional Moçambicana (Mozambique National Resistance)
RH	Reproductive Health
RUF	Revolutionary United Front
SAPs	Structural Adjustment Programmes
STDs	Sexually transmitted diseases
STIs	Sexually transmitted infections

UAPS	Union for African Population Studies
UN	United Nations
UNAFRI	United Nations African Institute for the Prevention of Crime and Treatment of Offenders
UNAIDS	Joint United Nations Programme on HIV and AIDS
UNDP	United Nations Development Programme
UNECA	United Nations Economic Commission for Africa
UNESCO	United Nations Educational, Scientific and Cultural Organization
UNFPA	United Nations Population Fund
UNHCR	United Nations High Commissioner for Refugees
UNICEF	United Nations Children's Fund
UNITA	União Nacional para a Independência Total de Angola (National Union for the Total Independence of Angola)
UNRISD	United Nations Institute for Social Development
VVF	Vesicular vagina fistula
WHO	World Health Organization
WSSD	World Summit for Social Development

1

Introduction

This focus of this book is on the challenges facing African families in the twenty-first century. Chapter 1 flags the central theme—that the family is the basic unit of society, and an enduring institution in Africa. To set the discussions that follow in proper perspective, Chapter 2 briefly discusses African families in an historical context, focusing especially on the colonial era. The functions and processes of formation of African families are then discussed in detail, outlining the ways in which families seek to maintain varying measures of solidarity among their members through the institution of marriage—the threshold to family formation. Chapter 3 reviews the context of childbearing, child-rearing and child fostering, and the importance of children to the survival of the lineage. The multiple roles played by Africa's women, and the ways in which education, employment and current economic conditions are reshaping these complex roles are also outlined in this chapter. In effect, the issues raised in these sections provide a backdrop for a discussion of the crises confronting African families and their members: children, adolescents and youths in particular. The changing context of African families is taken up in Chapter 4.

Globalization, conflicts and war, poverty and economic restructuring, rapid population growth, urbanization and migration, reproductive health, HIV/AIDS and harmful traditional practices, ageing, care and support of the elderly are among the key challenges confronting African families today. The effects of these challenges are discussed in Chapter 5. The vulnerability and resilience of African families in the face of crises and challenges are issues dealt with in Chapter 6. Chapter 7 presents the recommendations emanating from the study, which are aimed at strengthening the institution of the family—Africa's enduring and multifunctional unit. Finally Chapter 8 presents conclusions and a summary of the previous chapters.

Africa is a continent of contradictions: rich in resources, yet the worst affected by poverty. Wars, and civil and political destabilization, have severely eroded the developmental progress of the post-independence decades. In the present trend of globalization, Africa is the continent that is most disadvantaged; rather than being able to compete with the rest of the world, it has to grapple immediately with basic issues such as poverty, conflicts and the ravaging HIV/AIDS pandemic, all of which impact severely on the family. Yet African families remain resilient, even in the face of these crises.

The family is the basic unit of society in Africa, described by the United Nations (United Nations, 1991a) as 'the smallest democracy'. It is the primary unit responsible for family formation, contracting marriage, procreation and child rearing. As the primary socializing agents of society, African families function mainly as economic organs—both as units of production and of consumption. Apart from their basic functions as units of biological reproduction and intergenerational solidarity, families are also the main mechanism for social control and are the focus of most activities that permeate all aspects of African life, including religion and politics. It is therefore pertinent to position African families in an historical context in order to enhance our understanding of the present situation and of the challenges for the future.

2

African families: historical context, formation and functions

HISTORICAL CONTEXT

During the colonial period, African families were at the receiving end of a variety of policies—some persuasive, but mostly coercive or punitive. The same still obtains today, albeit to varying degrees. The forcible removal of families and communities from their ancestral homes and land by colonialists and settlers in Rhodesia (now Zimbabwe), South Africa, and South-West Africa (now Namibia) are illustrative of this. In West Africa, forced labour recruitment by French and Portuguese colonialists dislocated families as men were conscripted or forced to migrate to earn money to pay imposed taxes. This was also the case in South Africa, where taxes were imposed to force men to work in the mines and on white farms. Before then, internecine war for supremacy between kingdoms—for instance in Nigeria and Ghana—also served to dislocate families and their members (Amin, 1974). These wars also left their scars on the structure of families: for instance polygyny was a practical response to generally low sex ratios—there being more females than males—as well as a solution to the demand for family labour.

Colonial economic activities accentuated regional inequalities both within and between the countries of Africa. The establishment of European administrative networks was followed by contract and forced-labour legislation and agreements, and resulting recruitment. Forced-labour and a compulsory cash-cropping system were adopted by French colonialists in West Africa to obtain the vast labour force required for infrastructural work, especially for road and railway construction in the north, and for plantation agriculture in the coastal countries. An agreement in 1908 between the Portuguese administration and South Africa, and later a

3

decree in 1926, declared all unemployed adult males liable for contract labour for up to six months within Angola, or for six to twelve months outside the country. These laws sparked off large-scale clandestine emigration of unskilled adult males to neighbouring countries to escape forced-labour recruitment and the abuses associated with their implementation (Adepoju, 2003c[1]).

With time, the free migration of individuals and families in search of better living conditions increased. Young men from Upper Volta (now Burkina Faso), Mali, Niger, Chad and Guinea migrated to the mining and cocoa farms of Gold Coast (now Ghana), the plantations and forest industries of Ivory Coast (now Côte d'Ivoire) and the groundnut fields of Sene-Gambia. Circular migration in South Africa was engineered by laws which required migrant workers to leave their families at home. These men were accommodated mainly in appalling single-sex hostels, worked for the two years stipulated by the laws of contract labour, and returned to their families for as long as it was economically feasible, thereby greatly reducing the social costs normally sustained by receiving countries (Thahane, 1991). An average miner would make around a dozen such contract trips to the mines during his working life. Labour migration, dual residence of family members, female-headed households and so on were thus rooted in the colonial era.

FUNCTIONS OF THE FAMILY

The key functions of a family are to provide the basis of sexual activity, and to raise children and provide them with care, love, nurturing and discipline in a supportive environment. Further functions of the family, sometimes carried out in interaction with other institutions, include:

- Production activities (production, processing and marketing of goods and services)

- Home-making activities (cooking, cleaning, obtaining water, fuel and food)

- Learning activities (social and cultural norms and expectations, education, health and nutrition)

---

1.   Unless indicated as *Adepoju, Adunola*, all citings of *Adepoju* in this text refer to the author (given in the References as *Adepoju, Aderanti.*).

- Social activities (participation in social organizations)

- Cultural activities (participation in religious ceremonies)

- Transmission, preservation and change of values, communication, etc.

In essence, the family procreates, socializes and educates the children (Leiden-frost, 1992).

The predominance of subsistence economies in Africa's rural areas makes labour the crucial factor of production, for which families recruit from within themselves. In the African context, the household economy is intricately integrated into the family structure. The family is in many respects the basis of ownership of land and its management—an economic unit of production and consumption. Each family in the traditional setting is apportioned a piece of land for cultivation. Strangers are not entitled to such land but may cultivate it as share-croppers or tenant farmers. Traditionally, the women fetch firewood for cooking, and water for domestic use, and may also raise livestock in the yards. In that context also, the family has been the unit responsible for cultivation, family food security and management of the environment—functions sustained by the process of family formation.

FAMILY FORMATION

Traditionally, a family is assumed to evolve from marriage, and may vary from one culture to another in terms of size, composition and function. Unlike the theoretical 'life cycle approach', based on stages through which families are presumed to move, real life situations are complex, and include situations where men and/or women bring children into their first marriages. In addition, some marriages become polygynous, while others break up and the partners re-marry, so that residential locations are dispersed. These are only some of the complexities involved (Omideyi, 1992).

In themselves, families are not entities or agents; they are comprised of individuals who pass through a number of life stages, each of which is linked to what is expected of and is due to them. Consequently, any analysis of the family has to take into account the very different experiences of particular individuals (Adepoju, Adunola, 2001[2]). Definitions of the family and its component members—parent, wife, husband, and child—vary considerably from one context to another. The expectations and experiences of those roles can also differ over time.

Marriage, the cornerstone of the process of family-building in Africa, is a common event, and essentially a group activity. African societies insist on it as the threshold to family formation. A permanent state of celibacy is foreign to African cultures, being regarded as abnormal for men and unthinkable for normal, healthy women. Mate selection practices, either endogamous or exogamous, in the process of family formation in Africa, is largely a lineage affair. Although gradually crumbling under the weight of education, urbanization and migration, in some communities selection of mates is still largely a parental function. Men in Africa usually marry wives who are considerably younger than themselves, often of lower social and economic status.

Traditional marriage is the most common type, and the existence of different systems of family formation are usually functions of socio-cultural practices and economic circumstances. Entry into a union is an almost inevitable prospect for Africans, the advent of which can be hastened by unplanned pregnancy or delayed by the need for the man to accumulate bride-wealth (Locoh, 1988). Bride-wealth serves many purposes: it reinforces cultural norms, show-cases the economic and social standing of the suitor, creates customary bonds and friend-ship between the two families in question and gives the man's family some 'rights' over the woman, especially over her sexuality and fertility. In parts of Uganda, for example, the sex rights of the brother-in-law are seen as being partly justified by the bride-wealth paid out of the family central resource pool (Ntozi & Kabera, 1989). In many parts of Africa, dowry payment which marks the cere-monial beginning of family formation also discourages the dissolution of unions on other than serious grounds. The reason is that the prospect of returning the dowry is understandably hated.

Although there are variations between countries and over time, the age at marriage, particularly for females, is low, and so is the age at first pregnancy. In rural areas, nearly all females marry before their twenty-fifth birthday, and about 70 per cent are married before the age of twenty. On average, men in western and eastern Africa marry at around age 26, those in North Africa at around 27 and for those in the southern countries around 29 years (UNFPA, 1999). As marriages

2.   Unless indicated, as here, as *Adepoju, Adunola*, all citings of *Adepoju* in this text refer to the author (given in the References as *Adepoju, Aderanti.*).

come early in life for women, so does the onset of childbearing. In fact, it is generally believed that one of the fastest rewards of marriage is the birth of a child—so much so that a childless woman is regarded as a failure not only in marriage but also in life! The observed major determinants of the timing of marriage are religion, education of women and women's non-agricultural work patterns.

Several African governments stipulate a minimum age at marriage for girls, with or without parental consent. This is often as low as thirteen years in the former situation, and about eighteen in the latter. Traditionally, marriage is a major preoccupation for women and parents eagerly await the opportunity to marry off their daughters soon after they have reached puberty, which can be as early as fourteen years old or even less. By the age of fifty, over ninety percent of all African men and women have been married at least once. At that age also, about half of the women are no longer in their first union; two-thirds of the dissolutions are by separation or divorce, and one third of the women are widowed. The practice of levirate[3] helps to minimize the time spent by a widow outside of a marriage union (Locoh, 1988).

Although marriage and child-bearing start early, the termination of child-bearing does not necessarily coincide with the age of menopause. Among the Yorubas of Nigeria, for example, mothers do not bear children in competition with their married daughters. In a society in which many girls marry as early as age seventeen, the length of a generation can be short and hence child-bearing can cease at 30–35 years, thus providing a traditional check on fertility (Adepoju, 1977). In recent years, however, the spread of formal education and the access of girls to wage employment has delayed the age of entry into family formation and, therefore, timing of becoming a grandmother.

Polygamy and monogamy are the main forms of marriages. The proportion of women in polygamous marriages is highest in western Africa, and lowest in southern Africa (Mbugua, 1992). The prevalence of polygynous unions is associated with the levirate system, and the failure of a first wife to bear a (male) child (Chojnacka, 2000). In Muslim societies, the purdah system largely confines wives to their husbands' private compounds, and in Sudan and northern Nigeria, for instance, the shariah legal code has added new dimensions to the nature of sanc-

---

3.   The practice whereby a widow must be married by her late husband's brother or other near kinsman.

tions for infidelity and premarital sexual activity for women (though not for men). Polygamy has however been outlawed in Tunisia since the early 1960s.

3

The role of women in the family

CHILDBEARING, CHILD-REARING AND FOSTERING

Childbearing is a fundamental aspect of family life that is deeply rooted in African tradition, culture and religion. Women bear children early, often till late in their reproductive span. Since many of these children die due to poor health, medical and environmental conditions, poverty, taboos, infectious and communicable diseases, parents bear many children to ensure that at least some of them will survive.

High fertility permeates the fabrics of African society: the completed family size normally ranges from four to six children. Fertility is high even among educated people, who are usually regarded as small-family innovators. This is because fertility is determined by social values, attitudes and institutions, which could be affected by the process of modernization—urbanization, increasing literacy, rising expectations and aspirations—and by social and economic changes or other fundamental factors. Social roles, functions and relationships help to create a sense of belonging and purpose and are essential to family cohesion and continuity. Indeed, the dominant aspect of family functioning over the generations is that of procreation. Families strive to ensure that their girls get married early, and marriage is arranged between families, not individuals—in part to ensure their survival, as well as familial control. Young couples are encouraged to have children early in their marital life, and as many children as possible soon thereafter. The preference is for sons, to perpetuate the lineage and family name, and women who do not bear sons are either divorced or the husband is made to marry other wives until a male child is born.

In Africa, the value attached to having children is much more than the econo-mist's concept of children as consumption goods. As well as the survival of the lineage, children add to parental prestige, strengthen marital bonds, and guaran-tee old age security. Family size is one aspect of social structure which can hardly change in isolation. Very few of these strong traditional values have changed; indeed, the pressure on couples to have large families comes from parents and relations, or even from neighbours. In most cases, especially in the rural areas, the cost of child-rearing is shared by the extended families through child-fostering, thus relieving couples of the direct burden of large families. This caretaking includes feeding, providing shelter and clothing, as well as contributing to schooling expenditures, thereby spreading the cost of rearing children across a large group of people.

Child-fostering is a common practice in African families: poor families give out their children for nurturing and care, and better off families receive them (Isiugo-Abanihe, 1985). The willingness of many African families to delegate child care has been increased by the deteriorating economic fortunes of families in rural areas. Oppong and Abu (1987) reported, for instance, that in Ghana educated women were usually recipients of such children, sent to help in the home, to attend school or learn a trade. Infertile and sub-fertile women look for children to foster as a substitute for their own. In essence, separation of mother and child is a culturally-sanctioned practice in Africa. In these situations women constitute the anchor-points for families, through both procreation and child care.

THE CHANGING ROLE OF WOMEN

The African woman performs multiple roles—as daughter, sister, wife, mother, housekeeper, worker, kinswoman and citizen. In the traditional subsistence situa-tion, a woman's life is closely oriented towards her capacities to reproduce and provide subsistence for her family. If the records are reliable, it seems that, in spite of high parity[1] and a multiplicity of roles, the rate of female labour partici-pation outside the home remains high, but under-recorded. In many African societies, older relatives—grannies as well as older girls—cater for the young chil-dren thereby enabling mothers to concentrate fully on their economic activities, especially trading (Oppong, 1982).

---

1.   A demographic term meaning number of births

Within traditional African society, the family has been the major source of social status for women. A woman's status is largely a derived status: she is someone's wife, the mother of a son or daughter of her husband. Among the Igbos of Nigeria, the Swazi of Swaziland and the Dinkas of Sudan for instance, the value of the bride price often symbolizes the woman's status. Its persisting existence in the face of the increasingly 'modern' conjugal relationships is a good example of how the family still retains its grip on individuals.

Women's multiple roles as wives and mothers remain dominant, although differences in culture, tradition, religion, historical development, economic life and political systems are reflected in the extent of women's participation in various activities within their societies. Studies in western Africa, particularly in Ghana, confirmed this, indicating seven roles for women within the African family context: the parental role, the occupational role, the conjugal role, the domestic role, the kin role, the community role, and the individual role (Oppong and Abu, 1987).

This scenario is dynamic. Under the gender-based division of agricultural labour, both men and women take part in productive tasks. Cultural norms bestow a higher status on men than women, who combine domestic activities with a set of 'women's jobs' and the cultivation of 'women's crops'. In small-holding rural families, the 'feminization' of agriculture and the increasing dependence on female labour result in women being considerably overworked, especially as male labour becomes scarce owing to migration, conflicts and drought—as has happened in Lesotho, the Democratic Republic of Congo (DRC) and Ethiopia (Makinwa-Adebusoye, 1997). The greater the time and energy a woman devotes to farming, trading and other artisinal activities in order to increase her income, and the further she has to trek to fetch water and fuel wood for family sustenance, the less time and energy she has left to devote to caring for children, preparing nutritious meals, or making herself available for the healthcare of her family, and for family-planning clinics (Mbugua, 1997).

Economic transformation and male migration in search of employment have imposed on women an additional burden regarding the daily survival of their children. Education, economic deterioration, migration and individual aspirations are helping to redefine these roles. The concepts of gender equality and equity may not be relevant, suitable or appropriate and may need to be adapted to the context of African women's lives within their families. Armstrong (1997) reported that—in Zimbabwe for instance—women would forego autonomy, in terms of economic empowerment, if it meant that they would become socially alienated from members of their extended family.

The participation of women in various economic activities reflects prevailing culture, religion, economic life and political systems in society. Until recently, the bias rooted in the traditional gender roles limited the access of females to formal education, especially beyond the primary level. A series of socio-cultural constraints still inhibits the education of females beyond a particular level in various parts of the continent.

WOMEN'S EMPOWERMENT THROUGH EDUCATION AND EMPLOYMENT

Women are increasingly entering the waged-labour force. Access to education plays a major role, and diminishing family resources caused by unemployment and inflation have also rendered family incomes grossly inadequate for the sustenance of their members. In the past, women were expected to remain at home while their husbands worked to cater for the family. Nowadays both men and women must participate in economic activities, and women work hard, in addition to their domestic duties, to supplement whatever their husbands make from their employment.

Unable to gain better-paid formal sector employment, increasing numbers of women in Africa, particularly in West Africa, have turned to self-employment in the informal sector, either as a supplement to formal sector earnings or as the sole source of support (Oppong, 1992). The result is overwork and low pay for women and harder times for their families. Women work longer hours—doing housework, caring for children and preparing food. They have little or no access to vocational training and are in many cases precluded from participation in such programmes by educational prerequisites, timing conflicts between instruction hours and inflexible work and family responsibilities, as well as by distance and the lack of cheap transport.

African women occupy a central position in the production of goods and services. They perform the majority of the work in food processing and dominate both rural and urban informal sector activities. In many parts of Africa, women have been, and continue to be, responsible for much of the demanding agricultural tasks, especially weeding and harvesting. They combine these duties with the energy-sapping and time-consuming tasks of food processing, food preparation and the marketing of farm produce, conveyed from the farm to periodic markets over considerable distances.

As many male (head of household) workers have been retrenched, women bear the brunt of poverty within households and have had to combine several activities. Even those who are wage earners combine their work with petty trading, to make ends meet. As women bear larger proportions of household responsibilities, the need for them to work longer hours or undertake multiple activities, and for those hitherto unemployed to seek for work, has intensified.

The economic situation of women may be getting worse, given the current economic crisis. Economic downturn and social disintegration have reduced the resource base of many women's families and have shifted a larger share of the income-generating burden onto women (Mbugua, 1997). As the phenomenon of increasing proportions of single women—without husbands and kin to assist, control or protect them—becomes widespread, women are evolving a series of initiatives to survive the economic crisis and the prospect of a dismal future.

4

Crises and the changing structure of African families

Families globally, and African families in particular, are undergoing rapid transformation as a result of social change, modernization, the impact of the media and globalization, as well as because of poverty and economic crises. Warning signals on issues relating to refugee children, sexual exploitation, trafficking in children and the general health and welfare of children were given by the (then) OAU (Organization of African Unity) which, in 1990, expressed concern, saying that

> "Armed conflicts have increased in Africa. The number of African children caught up in wars and civil strife has tragically grown. Children and women have become the main victims. Children in very difficult circumstances include those that are abused, exploited, disabled, orphaned, neglected or in prison. Some are refugees; others are victims of AIDS" (OAU, 1994).

The situation has since deteriorated dramatically. The number of street children has multiplied in the face of deepening poverty; adolescents are traumatized by the inability of families to provide for their basic needs, and unemployment is increasingly driving youths into the hands of traffickers, criminals and drug syndicates. All these are threatening the authority and solidarity of African families.

The structure and dynamics of family formation in Africa are in a state for flux. New types of family forms are emerging, resulting in tensions and strains. A variety of marriages exists and other new forms (such as informal marriages and visiting marriages) are emerging as a result of migration, sub-fertility and levirate practice. Different types of households have also emerged, including single households, female-headed, child-headed and 'skip' households. The term 'skip household' is used in South Africa to describe households with one or two missing generations as a consequence of the AIDS epidemics (Ziehl, 2004).

SINGLE-, CHILD-, FEMALE- AND GRAND-PARENT-HEADED FAMILIES

The most obvious changes experienced by African families are structural changes. Dual families with a single head, which are bi-residential rather than co-residential, have emerged as a new version of the traditional polygamous family. These are based largely on the need to maximize income through participation in economic activities of all spouses and other adult family members. Families without adult male kin—those female-headed households where the males have migrated, died or simply absconded—have increased. Africa is also witnessing the spectacle of families being headed by children and/or grandparents as a result of very early pregnancy, the demise of the parental generation through armed conflict, and the scourge of HIV/AIDS. In spite of these problems, family obligations to their members remain strong.

The 'typical' nuclear family is a rare phenomenon in Africa and is an idea borrowed from western culture. The traditional extended family in large compounds and the typical nuclear family are fast becoming rare; yet the lineage still exerts a strong influence on families. In fact there is no such thing as a homogeneous African family: due to a variety of interlinked factors, families in Africa have taken many diverse forms. Sandwiched between tradition and modernity, African families continue to bear the burden of the stresses being experienced in the different economic, social, cultural, and political sectors of society. In the process the significance of families in Africa—in terms of their functions and responsibilities—has probably increased rather than decreased, even though the family remains the most fundamental and basic social unit.

This development necessitates innovative processes for adapting and adjusting to changes, pressures and constraints as conditions have worsened for many families, owing to lack of gainful employment and reductions in social expenditures by governments across the continent. Migrations and refugee movements add to family disintegration, and the burden on women. Many youths, who now roam the cities as family ties break down, face the risk of sexual exploitation, unwanted pregnancies and sexually transmitted infections (ICPD, 1994).

CHILD LABOUR

In the African cultural setting, especially in rural areas, a child is regarded as an economic asset and, from around age six, he or she is gradually integrated into the family's productive process and also performs domestic services—baby sitting, cooking, cleaning, washing, and other household chores—which usually absorb a large share of the family budget in rich and low fertility societies. In a traditional subsistence economy, labour is usually the only crucial factor of production, and children enter the family labour force and work for their parents until they marry and—in the case of boys—are given a share of the family farm.

In a traditional setting, parents often prefer to send girls (rather than boys) into domestic service and use the income they generate to finance the education of the boys. To many African families, what is dubbed child labour in the literature in many cases represents a situation where the assistance that children provide—child caring, herding and fetching water or fuel wood—releases the adults, especially women, to undertake more urgent and major tasks. Thus, in seasons when extra hands are needed, families see no contradiction in withdrawing girls from school so that they can help, because all children are considered a family resource at all times (Adepoju, 1997).

In spite of acceding to the various conventions designed to eliminate child labour, the practice is widespread in Africa as a result of generalized poverty and economic crisis. Investment in family members is made based on who is perceived to be most likely to bring the highest returns. In most cases, this boosts the biased family investment in education in favour of boys (Adepoju, 2005). Moreover, domestic work for children not enrolled in school or for drop-outs is an integral part of family upbringing strategies and survival mechanisms. Poor parents, especially in rural areas, facing difficult resource constraints, enlist their children in domestic work, hoping thereby to diversify the family income. But fostered children and domestic workers, mostly young girls who wish to learn a trade or attend school, may be constrained by an exploitatively heavy work schedule.

In much of Africa's urban areas, many working boys are newspaper sellers, shoe-shiners and parking boys, working to support poor parents. Poverty is often the major factor forcing these young children into work. The first evidence of unemployment came not from statistics but from the appearance in the towns of people who obviously had nothing to do. They came in increasing numbers, and lived in shanty towns, in desperation and poverty.

STREET CHILDREN

In many sub-Saharan African countries, poverty is a major factor forcing young children into work. Street children as beggars are increasing in number in cities like Addis Ababa, Dakar, Nairobi and so on. These include children who simply work on the streets but are without families or homes (Moore, 1994). Some of them might have fled from home, lured by peers who live on the street independent of parental control. Others may be running away from parental abuse. In Senegal, such children are forced by religious leaders to beg in the streets for food and money. Often compelled to leave home because their parents are unable to cater for the needs of their families, street children experience harsh conditions while living off the streets, begging, searching garbage dumps, and sleeping under bridges in cold conditions. Their lifestyle makes them susceptible to sexually transmitted infections, especially HIV/AIDS. Most street children are sexually active, with some engaging in multiple partnerships and unprotected sex. Street children who use drugs increase their health risks and may be more prone to violence (Aderinto, 2003).

Children on the streets are vulnerable to exploitation from adults and are easily drawn into prostitution, drug-taking, alcohol abuse and crime. Products of famine, armed conflicts, rural-urban migration, unemployment, poverty and broken families, such children constitute a growing urban tragedy with a negative impact on civil social structure. They are often exposed to brutal treatment by security guards and the police and consequently move around in gangs which give a measure of protection and a sense of belonging and commitment. Prostitution is often a common way for boys and girls on the street to make money. In Nairobi, for example, such girls may be selling sexual services during the day and returning to their 'community' at night (Moore, 1994). Sexually transmitted infections are a major health problem, and girls are vulnerable to sexual violence and exploitation. The culture of violence, petty crime and substance abuse reflects the harshness and brutality of the circumstances that these street children, dislodged from their families, have to cope with, as well as the daily problem of having to make ends meet.

AFRICA'S ADOLESCENTS

In July 1987, the African Heads of State declared 1988 the year for the protection, survival and development of Africa's children. This move, based on the Bamako Initiative, proposed that maternal and child health care should be made available to the whole continent by the mid-1990s. Today, many African countries are unable to adequately feed, educate or clothe their teeming populations or provide adequate shelter and health facilities—the basic needs required for decent livelihood.

Among adolescents (age 10–19 years), girls are particularly vulnerable members of African families. Faced with discriminative practices—cultural, institutional, and legal—they are often denied equal access to educational opportunities and may be forced to marry at a very early age, usually to men considerably older than themselves. By bearing children early, the adolescent girl exposes herself to a series of health problems, including sexually transmitted infections and vesicular vagina fistula (VVF). Lacking information, knowledge and access to family planning, by age twenty-five she may already have had five or even six children.

Adolescent pregnancies are now pervasive in societies which previously had strong traditional prescriptions against premarital childbearing. Age at marriage has increased in several African countries, as has the incidence of 'baby mothers', abandoned babies and deaths among pregnant adolescents through illegal abortions. Yet most population policies and programmes in Africa still frown at providing contraceptive information and supplies to adolescents. In a United Nations survey, it was found that one third of the 18 African countries with family planning programmes did not provide contraceptives to unmarried teenagers, and only one country in five indicated that family life education is included in school curricula (United Nations, 1989). Yet adolescent girls, married or unmarried, contribute the greatest proportion of gynaecological emergencies. At delivery they suffer from medical complications including anaemia, premature delivery, prolonged labour, cervical trauma, even death. This development is increasingly visible in both rural and urban areas, but is more evident in the towns, where family and social controls on adolescents have weakened considerably over the past decade or so.

Those institutions that have the potential to ameliorate the situation of African adolescents are themselves contributing to an aggravation of the problem. The majority of schools in Africa are intolerant of schoolgirl pregnancies and prohibit such girls from continuing with their formal education—at a time when they need education most. A study carried out in Kenya in 1988, for instance, established that about 8000 teenagers were forced to drop out of school that year because of adolescent pregnancy. Similarly in Tanzania about 18, 800 primary and secondary school students were expelled from school in 1984 due to pregnancy (Mbugua, 1992). Those responsible for the pregnancy—boy-students, older men and even male-teachers—go scot-free, no doubt to repeat their nefarious actions.

AFRICA'S YOUTH

Youths are usually defined as those in the age group 10–24 years, a definition that overlaps with adolescents, but in the African context, youths often remain under parental care and surveillance until they marry and/or establish an independent means of livelihood. All over Africa, young people are sandwiched between the family and the state, between tradition and modernity and are inadequately prepared for the transition from childhood to youth and scarcely aware of their responsibilities as parents. Illiteracy, lack of educational opportunities, a high drop-out rate and unemployment are among the daunting problems faced by Africa's youths. Fewer girls than boys have access to schools and far fewer complete their courses. Girls who drop out marry and become mothers, only to repeat the poverty syndrome; uneducated girls are severely disadvantaged in the marriage and employment markets.

Unemployment in Africa's urban areas is essentially among the youth. Initially, localized among primary school leavers in the early 1960s, the pool of the unemployed now includes both secondary school leavers and university graduates. The unemployed youth, on whose education parents and society expended scarce financial resources, remain socially and economically dependent, and disillusioned. To the extent that economic and social crises prevent the family from adequately fulfilling its customary role, young Africans find themselves torn between traditional and western systems, neither of which can fulfill their aspirations and expectations.

For most youths, the perceived solution is migration, either in pursuit of higher education or for employment, initially towards the towns and very possibly from there to other countries. For a few, such migration is of the mobility type, but for the large majority it is strictly for survival (Adepoju, 2001). Worsening youth unemployment and rapidly deteriorating socio-political and economic conditions, poverty and human deprivation, stimulated and intensified irregular migration as well as trafficking in young boys and girls. A few years ago a young graduate would secure a job, establish an independent household soon after graduating from the university, marry and raise a family and begin a process of assisting siblings to acquire formal education. Today a young graduate can roam the streets, seeking for a job for months without success, and even if he or she is successful, his or her salary is likely to be too meagre to support a minimum level of living. In desperation most of these youths risk everything to fight their way hazardously to the countries of the North, with the assistance of traffickers and bogus agencies, in search of the illusory greener pastures (Adepoju, 2005).

Trafficking in children and adults

A variety of factors, including deepening poverty, deteriorating living conditions, persistent unemployment, conflicts, human deprivation, and a feeling of dismal future have fostered the conditions for human trafficking to flourish in Africa (Salah, 2004). Child trafficking is a serious human rights issue but the problems of child abuse and neglect are rooted primarily in the deteriorating economic situation. Deepening rural poverty forces poor families to give up their children to traffickers, under the pretext of providing them the opportunity of securing good jobs and better lives. Poverty, lack of access to education, unemployment, family disintegration as a result of death or divorce and neglected AIDS-orphaned children, make young people vulnerable to traffickers (Adepoju, 2005; Moore, 1994). These traumatic developments reflect the depth of the deterioration of the region's economies and the increase in poverty (ILO 2003).

The inability of parents to pay the fees for their wards' education is exploited by traffickers to lure young girls with offers of education and employment opportunities elsewhere (Adepoju, 2005). In Togo, for instance, child trafficking begins with a private arrangement between an intermediary and a family member, with promises of education, employment or apprenticeship, which only turn out to be exploitative jobs as domestic workers. Sometimes, parents have had to pay an intermediary to find work for their children; in a number of cases parents accepted money from traffickers, paid as inducements for the transaction.

In Africa, child rearing has traditionally been a shared communal responsibility, particularly in close-knit rural areas. As children who provide help in the home and on the farm are enrolled in schools, especially in the cities, this resource disappears from the family pool. This is evidenced by the case of Gabon where compulsory schooling and strict labour laws have created a huge demand for domestic labour. A survey of 600 working children in Gabon in 1998–1999 found that only 17 were Gabonese. In 2001, between 10 000 and 15 000 trafficked Togolese girls were working in Gabon. They were recruited as domestic servants by agents who paid their poor parents, and transported them for domestic work (UNICEF, 2000).

Child trafficking in Africa is a demand-driven phenomenon: the existence of an international market for children in labour and the sex trade, coupled with an abundant supply of children from poor families with limited or no means of education in a cultural context that favours child fostering (ILO, 2003). Child trafficking has also increased as a result of a growing network of intermediaries, the absence of any clear legal framework, the scarcity of trained police to investigate cases of trafficking, ignorance and complicity by parents, corruption of border officials, and open borders that make the control of transnational movement an intractable problem (Salah, 2004).

With regard to women, the literature also indicates that they often fall prey to traffickers as a result of poverty, rural-urban migration, unemployment, broken homes, displacement and peer influence. Poverty is the major reason for trafficking in women. Unemployment, low wages and poor living standards drive some desperate women into the hands of traffickers. These women then end up offering sexual services in brothels, or as domestic servants. Poor women who wish to migrate to rich countries may simply be looking for better job opportunities in order to assist their families. In the process, some fall prey to traffickers. Though some of the trafficked women are willing to participate in prostitution in order to escape the poverty trap, deception is the most common strategy used in procuring women and young girls through offers of further education, marriage and remunerative jobs. The trafficked people, who obtain huge loans for procuring their tickets, visas and accommodation, find on arrival that the promises were bogus, and their passports are seized to forestall their escape (Adepoju, 2005). Many of these women are stranded and helpless, but the absence of any judicial framework limits attempts by law enforcement agencies to prosecute and punish perpetrators and their accomplices for trafficking crimes.

These days many women are assuming sole responsibility for family members when their husbands die of AIDS. Saddled with increased responsibilities, some may opt for migration in search of employment to improve their families' well-being only to fall prey to traffickers. Sexual exploitation may also expose such women to HIV/AIDS infection. Trafficked women in the sex trade often work without the use of condoms and may be forced to lower their prices for sexual services to pay off their debt bondage. Some may be raped, tortured and subjected to other forms of inhumane physical abuse by clients and traffickers. Repatriated women arriving back in Nigeria through Lagos are forced to undergo medical tests, including tests for HIV/AIDS, as part of a screening process (Pearson, 2002). Their re-integration back home when deported is made difficult by the stigma of failure, and local communities are wary of repatriated victims who may spread diseases contracted abroad. Many such victims of trafficking end up engulfed in, rather than escaping from the trap of poverty, bringing in its wake personal trauma and dishonour to their families.

HIV/AIDS can in itself be both a cause and a consequence of trafficking. In southern Africa, for example, the perception that having sexual intercourse with a young girl diminishes a man's risk of contracting HIV/AIDS has increased demand for young sex-workers, and unscrupulous traffickers are cashing on this situation by bringing young girls to the area. It has been found that some of the trafficked girls from Benin and Togo, who travel by sea to Gabon through transit points in south-eastern Nigeria, were raped, while a few prostituted themselves or sold their belongings in order to survive while awaiting their boats. Many died when these rickety boats capsized. At the destination, many girls suffered physical and emotional abuse and sexual exploitation by boys and men in the hosts' homes—experiences that pushed some to the streets as prostitutes. In spite of the risks, few insisted on the use of condoms because clients pay more for unprotected sex, exposing the women to HIV infection (Nagel, 2000; Human Rights Watch, 2003).

5

Challenges facing African families

As African families grapple with the myriad of crises engulfing their members, other challenges wrought on the family by external and internal dynamics have since metamorphosed. The principal challenges facing African families today include the unending cycle of violent conflicts, poverty, the impact of globalization, the onslaught of the media blitz on youth, rapid population growth, urbanization and migration, the reproductive health of its members, the impact on them of the HIV/AIDS pandemic, and the care and support of their aged in a situation of dwindling resources.

CONFLICT AND ITS EFFECTS ON FAMILIES

During the last two decades, Africa has been the most conflict-affected region in the world. Between 1980 and 2002, for instance, eleven of the most war-torn countries were in Africa, including Liberia, Rwanda, Angola, Mozambique, Côte d'Ivoire, Sierra Leone and Somalia; these were ranked amongst the most deadly conflict zones or countries in the world. At present there are more than twelve conflicts in Africa, ranging from the sporadic urban violence in many countries to decades-old wars and conflicts in Algeria, Angola, Burundi, Congo, Democratic Republic of Congo, Guinea Bissau, Ethiopia, Eritrea, Liberia, Mozambique, Sierra Leone, Sudan and recently Côte d'Ivoire. These conflicts have had a profound impact on the family, with far-reaching effects on its solidarity and functions.

In Angola, Liberia, Mozambique and Sierra Leone, the basic infrastructure—schools, hospitals, and homes—was devastated by war, and members of families were destabilized. A generation of children is now growing up in these

23

countries without the basic necessities of life. In fact a major adverse and endur-ing effect of the civil conflicts in several countries in Africa—Liberia, Uganda, Sudan, Mozambique, Sierra Leone, Angola—is that 'children have grown up more able to recognize the sound of each different gun than the alphabet, and are destined to remain illiterate and destitute' (United Nations, 2002b). Family for-tunes have similarly been wiped out.

One of the immediate consequences of the conflicts and wars in Africa is the bur-den of the maimed (as in Sierra Leone) and the disabled that is placed on families, since the rehabilitation of such people by government is far from adequate. The maiming continues even in those countries where the fighting has abated—because of the types of weapon used during the conflict, the most dan-gerous being land mines and similar anti-personnel devices (Adekanye, 1998; Colleta et al, 1996). The millions of land mines planted all over the countryside, for instance in Angola and Mozambique, continue to pose major treats to fami-lies and civilian population years after hostilities have ceased and complicate the task of providing aid to war victims. This also hinders the return of refugees to their traditional occupation—farming. So, many innocent victims such as chil-dren, women and the elderly continue to suffer the effects of the land mines and, with no compensation forthcoming from the government, it remains the respon-sibility of family members to look after such victims as best as they can.

CULTURE OF VIOLENCE

There are, however, more insidious and longer-term effects of war on families, the consequences of which will be felt perhaps for generations to come. The accli-matization of youths to violence is one of such distressing consequences (United Nations, 2001b).

While death used to be believed to have been appeased by prolonged mourning by entire communities for the loss of one of its members, deaths resulting from conflicts and wars are now commonplace. In the 1994 genocidal conflict in Rwanda, for example, children were forced to witness the killing of their parents and siblings, and rape was so widespread that nine months later abandoned babies filled up orphanages in the predominantly Catholic country where access to abortion is difficult. Such widespread killing and the abandoning of babies runs counter to strongly-held African family values. The future implications for victims can only be imagined.

ABANDONED 'WAR' CHILDREN

Many children were born to women abducted during period of conflict. Combatants often abandon their wartime families to reunite with their original families once they are demobilized at the end of conflicts. In Mozambique, Liberia, Sierra Leone and Uganda the number of children from such wartime unions is estimated to be in the thousands. Under pressure to rebuild their destroyed infrastructure, few governments emerging from periods of prolonged conflict are inclined—or even able—to address such social issues. Families or relatives are therefore saddled with the burden of rehabilitating such women and their babies from their own meagre resources (United Nations, 2001b).

CHILD SOLDIERS

The conscription of children as child-soldiers in the theatres of war in Africa is commonplace. National armies and—especially—rebel soldiers use children as human shields and combatants in conflict situations (Crisp, 2000). Many children lost their lives and limbs through being used as shields, especially among the rebels of the Lord's Resistance Army (LRA) in Uganda and the Revolutionary United Front (RUF) in Sierra Leone. Children have become one of the main targets of violence and in turn are being used to perpetuate it. Children are deliberately indoctrinated into a culture of violence and used as a specific instrument of war. Militia groups and irregular armed forces such as the LRA in Uganda, and others in Rwanda and in the Democratic Republic of Congo, the RUF in Sierra Leone, UNITA in Angola and former RENAMO in Mozambique, were noted for forcibly recruiting children and initiating them through acts of violence against their own community. The intention of these groups was to create a fighting force that is reckless towards civilians and believed to have a tactical advantage over conventional forces. Of the approximately 350 000 child soldiers worldwide, 200 000 are believed to be in Africa (United Nations, 2002a).

Child soldiers assume particular importance within the context of the family in war-affected countries such as Liberia, Sierra Leone, Côte d'Ivoire, Uganda, Somalia, Sudan and Mozambique. These children are often the product of violence themselves, having witnessed the violent death of one or both parents, siblings or other kin members. As a result, they have grown up feeling rejected and alienated and, with no family ties or support, have turned to violence, drugs and delinquency. Since most are orphaned, they have survived on their own in the bush for years, missing out on education and losing touch in their formative years with societal values and norms. Their future is bleak indeed. They represent a new phenomenon in Africa: a generation virtually de-linked from the nurturing and loving custody of their families. Policies and development efforts now have to contend with these children and their specific problems.

FAMILIES, REFUGEES AND DISPLACED PERSONS

War and internal conflicts and environmental disasters have generated millions of refugees, and continue to uproot and displace people in Africa. The cyclical famines, drought and desertification of 1973–74, 1984–85, 1990–92, 1994 and 2002 triggered waves of environmentally displaced persons in the Sahelian region of West Africa and in southern and eastern Africa. Most family herds of cattle were wiped out, people lost their jobs and savings, and families were forced from the parched countryside to towns in search of food and livelihood (Findley, 1997). The drought severely affected local economies, families and people's lives in Zambia, Ethiopia, Zimbabwe and South Africa.

In the process of flight, families who lose all or most of their belonging, property and land are forced to depend either on local hospitality—if they settle spontaneously among kith and kin across the borders—or on food aid if they are forced to live in refugee camps. Family members are often separated, with young men away fighting at the war front or killed, leaving children, women and old men in the camps. In the process the family as an organization is severely disrupted. Africa's refugee situation has been and remains a human tragedy in both magnitude and complexity (Kibreab, 1983; United Nations, 2002a). The poorest of all regions, Africa accommodates about 7 million refugees and more internally displaced people, mostly children and women who migrate from one poor country to another already plagued with famine, war and drought. Many countries are locked in recurrent internal instability and ethnic, religious or related conflicts, resulting in disruptive population displacements. Wars and civil unrest generate refugees as political destabilization severely erodes progress in the post-independence decades.

The refugee situation in Africa is fluid: while old problems that gave rise to refugees are being solved, new problems have surfaced, intensifying the refugee crisis in countries such as Liberia, Sierra Leone, Guinea, Democratic Republic of

Congo, Congo, Côte d'Ivoire, Burundi, Rwanda and Sudan. Countries that generate large numbers of refugees also provide asylum for refugees from neighbouring countries. Virtually all refugees are confined to the continent, and are in the first instance assisted by fellow African families—a process facilitated by ethnic and kinship ties between refugees and people in their countries of asylum (Adepoju, 1989). As armed conflicts have intensified, the number of children caught up in wars and civil strife has tragically grown, with children, women and the elderly as the main victims, especially in new refugee-generating countries.

The number of internally displaced persons escalates daily, as millions are forced to seek refuge in neighbouring countries. Some fleeing from persecution and violence, natural disaster, drought, ecological problems, and internal conflict are displaced within their own countries. These include children, women and old people, mostly of rural background in countries which are ecologically fragile and where the rapidly encroaching desert forces populations to abandon their traditional pastoral or peasant agricultural base and migrate to the coastal regions of their respective countries (RPG, 1992). Others remain traumatized, being forced to live near the sites of such tragedies.

Refugees are often settled in artificial environments rather than in communities which function normally. Given the gender imbalance in refugee camps, social relations become distorted (Martin, 1991). Often marriages are no longer arranged as traditional family affairs; divorce tends to be high, and social norms and values are disrupted. The loss of the extended family and its traditional base for the care of the disabled, old people and orphans frequently results in trauma and rejection for those affected.

Apart from the initial trauma, the dangers, uncertainties and risks associated with life in refugee camps are overwhelming. Refugees are often insecure physically, socially, emotionally and spiritually. This is especially the case where the initial traditional local support and hospitality turn sour. Resentment from the local recipient population can hinder effective integration—as was the case with the Rwandan refugees in 1994 in Tanzania, a country reputed for its traditional hospitality to refugees (Blavo, 1999). In the absence of opportunities for gainful employment in the camps, men lose self-respect and dignity; women are exposed to gender and sexual violence, including rape, as well as the daily struggle to keep their tattered families together. The reproductive health conditions of refugees and displaced persons are often not promptly or even adequately addressed.

It has been suggested that most conflicts in Africa result from poverty, lack of respect for human rights, bad governance, corruption, and a struggle for control of centrally-dominated national resources (Adekanye, 1998). Globalization, some argue, can open a window of opportunity by linking local markets to international ones, and by generating employment to alleviate poverty.

AFRICAN FAMILIES IN A GLOBALIZING MARKET

Africa is marginalized in the global market and globalization has exposed many countries of the continent to global risks and uncertainties, thereby increasing their vulnerability (Abdellaziz, 2003). Owing to incessant conflicts and distorted macro-economic conditions, little direct foreign investment has been attracted to create jobs and reduce poverty. Archaic information technology reinforces the lack of ability of domestic enterprises to compete in the global market.

Globalization has been defined as the process of growing economic interdependence of countries in the international economy, fostering international financial flows, rapid diffusion of technology, and institutional linkages between firms in different countries. Deepening integration of trade, markets and finance are resulting in increasing interdependence, sustained by a liberalization of economic policies—deregulation and privatization activities, and the removal of cross-border impediments to the flow of financial services, trade, transportation, and communication. Global markets, global resources, global ideas and global solidarity can, as the 1999 Human Development report emphasized, enrich the lives of people everywhere (UNDP, 1999). The challenge is to ensure that benefits derivable from globalization are shared equitably and that interdependence works for people not just for profits.

In reality, however, globalization, driven by competitive global markets, is outpacing the governance of markets and undermining human development. Indeed, globalization and so-called liberation have generated severe contradictions and have, for a variety of reasons, not benefited Africa, which has not been adequately incorporated into the global economy. Many African countries have lowered their tariff regimes and promoted free trade without a corresponding inflow of foreign direct investment to stimulate job creation. Therein lies the contradiction: globalization implies free movement of capital and information, but at the same time movement of people is curtailed. Yet migration is increasingly becoming part of the global process of communication and information flows.

The disadvantageous position of African countries in the new era of globalization impacts on the family in various ways. Firstly, agricultural subsidies in the USA and Europe are impacting negatively on the income of farmers in Africa. One particular instance is the billions of dollars paid to the small number of cotton growers in the USA which has drastically affected the livelihood of 10 million cotton growers and their families in Mali, Burkina Faso, Kenya, Ghana and so on. Most of these people are now migrating to the cities, in a desperate bid for survival. Secondly, restrictions on migration to developed countries are forcing young people to enlist the services of bogus agents, thus increasing illegal migration and curtailing potentials for remittances from migrants which help to sustain poor families. Also—as estimated by the World Bank—high tariffs and technical barriers to trade cost sub-Saharan African countries about US$20 billion yearly in lost exports—much-needed revenue which could have been used for development and employment generation. The general consensus is thus that globalization has impoverished Africa and its component units, the family in particular.

The internet has exerted tremendous impact, both positive and negative, on information flows across the globe. African families have undergone considerable transformation in their structure, nature and function, due to both external influences and internal dynamics. The new socialization processes for young people and the heterogeneous contexts (globalization, education, mass media, religious fundamentalism etc.) in which they find themselves have led to the erosion of traditional norms and bonds. Increased contact with the world has opened the family to new norms and values, some productive and others inimical to African cultures.

The unprecedented and powerful impact of both electronic and print media have been profound. In many cases the traditional values and norms of African families and societies are challenged regarding issues like homosexuality, same-sex marriages, nudity and a barrage of pornographic materials, violent and X-rated films and similar materials that are readily accessible to vulnerable young people via the internet. This is particularly worrying as there are few regulatory authorities to screen either internet paedophiles or imported films which could destroy the very fabric of African cultural norms and values. At the moment, globalization has impacted on adolescents' mode of dressing and this is evidenced by the new fashion of scanty dressing of girls. The African family and its values are seriously threatened.

ECONOMIC RESTRUCTURING, POVERTY AND SURVIVAL STRATEGIES

Poverty is pervasive in Africa and is at the root of many problems confronting African families today. In many African countries, poverty is generally concentrated among people with low education, unstable employment or unemployment, low-status jobs, low and unstable income, poor housing conditions and large families. The incidence, depth and severity of poverty in African countries have tasked to the limit the ability of extended families to serve as safety net. Different manifestations of poverty are both widespread and severe among all sections of the population but especially among women and children, who are the most vulnerable groups. Illiteracy also plays a significant part. Rapid growth of population and labour force, combined with stagnant economic growth rates, have resulted in intensified poverty and unemployment.

The most pervasive effect of poverty on women is the additional burden and pressure of sustenance for their families: as poverty deepens and becomes more widespread, women are constantly under pressure—more than men are as husbands, fathers, and brothers. In the last two decades, mass retrenchment, belt-tightening fiscal policies to counter deteriorating economic conditions and high inflation have forced women to share the role of principal provider, previously preserved for men, or to assume that responsibility entirely. Over time, this near-reversal of traditionally assigned roles has almost become the norm.

In many African countries, the already poor social conditions of families are rendered poorer by 'stabilization and adjustment' measures. At the macro level, African families have borne the brunt of government reductions in spending on the social sectors. Access to education, health and other social services has been curtailed, thus reducing the overall welfare of the family as a unit—particularly the poorer ones. In the course of implementing Structural Adjustment Programmes (SAPs), attendance dropped dramatically in most hospitals in Ghana, Nigeria, Senegal, Tanzania, Zambia and a host of other countries, at least in part as a result of the cost recovery programmes. Poor patients, unable to pay stipulated fees have resorted to other, less efficient forms of health care. In Tanzania, for example, before SAPs were introduced, 90 per cent of women gave birth in clinics. Afterwards only 40 per cent could afford to do so (Adepoju, 1996). As subsidies were withdrawn from staple food (maize in Zambia and Zimbabwe, rice in Liberia and wheat in Senegal) and social services (health, education and public transportation in particular), workers were hard pressed to meet daily family obligations. It is now common in many capital cities to see hundreds of workers trekking on foot, morning and evening, to and from their offices, or to discover people, children included, making do with only one meal a day.

Families have developed a variety of survival strategies for their various members, ranging from selective migration to differential investment in education. In the context of structural adjustment, African families, acting as the safe haven of last resort, have had to provide social security for their retrenched members and sustain large numbers of out-of-work able-bodied men and women. Official social safety nets to ameliorate some of the negative impact of the restructuring programmes are little more than a palliative, essentially of a short-term nature and do not cover more than a small fraction of these workers affected.

The combined effects of devalued national currency, massive retrenchment of workers, declining real wages for those few still on the job, and inflation have intensified the sufferings of families already bearing the brunt of the adverse effects of SAPs. One of the most noticeable effects is the increased workload that women have had to bear, in both rural and urban areas. The tremendous increase in women's work has seriously compromised their ability to perform their traditional family welfare, health care and nurturing roles (Adepoju, 1996). A large proportion of poor women are increasingly being pushed into the labour force on very disadvantageous terms, due to the lowering of household incomes as real wages fall, unemployment rises and as remittances or supplementary incomes from migrant or resident husbands become inadequate for household consumption needs. The emergence of families of beggars who join the hordes of street children in urban areas of Tanzania, Nigeria, Ethiopia and Senegal is a manifestation of how widespread poverty has altered the values of Africans (Campbell and Ntsabane, 1995; Togonu-Bickersteth et al, 1997).

Often young girls—the mothers of tomorrow—are withdrawn from school because, with a diminished household income, their parents choose to educate only their brothers. Young girls may also be withdrawn from school because their families require their labour to help mothers and aunts in the face of dwindling family labour pool and the high cost of hired labour. SAPs have significantly impacted women's roles as producers, mothers, household managers and community organizers, impoverishing many women and perpetuating an intergenerational cycle of poverty.

FAMILIES IN AN URBANIZING SPACE

Compared with other major world regions, Africa has one of the lowest proportions of the population living in urban areas. This is estimated at 35 percent, ranging from 22 per cent in East Africa to 48 percent in southern Africa. Although Africa is predominantly a rural continent, by 2015, fifty per cent of its population will be urban (United Nations, 1998). The effects of this transformation on the living conditions of families, and the health and employment of its members could be dramatic. At the moment, migration and poverty and forced population movements are straining the capacity of the already overstretched support of extended families.

From a residential perspective, urbanization, migration and education dislodge family members. Residential patterns of African families have changed in response to education, migration and diminishing landholdings in rural areas. For newly married couples, residence is now dictated by the husband's employment and economic activities, as women tend to follow husbands. Urban areas attract working age members of the families particularly males but, increasingly, females are also moving from their rural homes in search of employment. Schooling separates children from their parents and from one another for prolonged periods of time as children are often sent to better-off relatives in towns, where post-primary schools are located.

Migration has led to the emergence of dual households for many African families. Migrants are predominantly male, and of an age where the process of family formation is at its peak. In most parts of Africa, rural-urban migration is actively pursued in search of greater prospects for gainful employment, education, self-reliance and progress (Adepoju, 2001). Because of increasing regional disparities within African countries, intra-regional migration has taken root. Since migration is generally spurred by adverse conditions in the migrants' place of origin, and may entail long durations of stay, the increasing tendency is for migrants to maintain two homes: one in their source area and the other at the destination, whether urban or rural (Mbugua, 1992). The reasons for maintaining dual homes include the need to maintain landed property in the source area; the obligation to care for aged parents and the need to maintain close links with relatives. Such dual residence can weaken conjugal bonds and the effective control of children, especially male children. Prolonged spousal separation may decrease the fertility[1] of the wife at source, as is the case in southern Africa's migrant labour system. The migrant's wife may also achieve greater autonomy and become more of a decision-maker.

Female-headed families are more common in western, eastern and southern Africa than in northern Africa. For instance, in the mid-1990s, thirty percent of households in Ghana and 35 percent in Kenya were headed by females. In southern Africa in particular, male migration to South Africa's mines from neighbouring countries is a major contributor to female-headed households (Isiugo-Abanihe and Obono, 1999). Out-migration of the male heads and widowhood may also lead to a higher incidence of female headship. Female heads who are widows are usually older than average, and are likely to have a large number of grandchildren residing with them. In urban areas female-headship is largely a function of polygamy without co-habitation. Oppong and Abu (1987) observed that in Ghana highly educated women, in the pursuit of education and professional careers, generally postpone marriage and are more likely to find suitable mates later on from the pool of married men.

Migration in Africa remains very much a 'family matter', with even non-migration family members intimately involved in and affected by the migration process. Decisions about who should migrate, where they should go to, and for how long, are therefore still sanctioned, if not completely controlled, by the family (Adepoju, 1990). This situation promotes the intergenerational flow of resources within the family through migrants' remittances, which constitute a lifeline for many poor families. Many parents, including migrants, resident in or out of Africa, insist that their children speak the language of their 'origin' even when these children may never get to know the place from which their parents originated.

---

1.   It should be understood that, in this context, the word 'fertility' refers to number of children actually born to a woman, rather than 'fecundity', the physical ability to bear children.

EDUCATION AND THE CHANGING DYNAMICS OF FEMALE MIGRATION

There is scant information available about female migration, a situation which derives from the numerical preponderance of males in the migratory streams; the 'invisibility' of women who, as wives, accompany migrant males (family migration) or join them (marriage migration). For many years migration surveys simply did not ask women about their migration experiences. Where women did move, it was assumed that this was associational—for marriage or to join family members (Makinwa-Adebusoye, 1990). This stereotype was later questioned and current surveys are confirming that economic concerns now play an important role in female migration decisions, even when women are joining a spouse.

Traditionally, men migrate leaving their wives and children (who may subsequently join them) in the care of the extended family. A variety of customs restricts female migration, as does job segregation and discrimination in the urban labour market. Two decades of economic distress and the changing economic circumstances are however increasingly forcing communities to condone the largely new phenomenon of female migration.

Women's work outside the home has become necessary as a result of the inability of men to cope with family demands. Before the ongoing economic crisis deepened, women supplemented husbands' income and remittances. As men increasingly lose their jobs, and incomes become irregular, rural women, like men, are turning to migration to urban areas to meet their economic obligations (Oppong, 1997). Women are also taking advantage of the expansion of employment opportunities in the urban formal and informal sectors, and this has encouraged their migration to the towns. Independent female migration directed toward attaining economic independence through self-employment or wage income is intensifying.

Increasing access to education by females means that educated women now have greater opportunities for employment in the urban formal sector and are able to compete and participate increasingly, and more effectively, in both non-domestic and formal sector activities (UNFPA, 2002). The increasing proportion of educated females is also reflected in the accelerated migration of women—especially young women—into urban areas to seek further education and jobs. These women are now also migrating internationally in search of greener pastures. This phenomenon is intensifying as men are at the same time gradually taking over work in crafts and services, thereby eroding a traditional domain of female employment. Women are more exposed, are demanding equal access to education and employment and no longer terminate their education in the kitchen as was hitherto the usual practice.

A significant proportion of educated women—single and married alike—migrate alone to developed countries in search of greener pastures. Once set in motion, the migration of skilled female migrants took root and is no longer confined to national borders. Female nurses and doctors have been recruited from Nigeria, Malaŵi, Zimbabwe, Ghana and South Africa to work in the UK (Buchan & Dovlo, 2004). Others migrate with their children to pursue their studies abroad since the educational system in many African countries has virtually collapsed. Thus, in a reversal of traditional gender roles, independent female migration is leading to a situation where the men are left at home to look after the children (Adepoju, 1995). To the extent that this is a relatively new phenomenon, it constitutes an important change in gender roles.

Increasing female migration may be a reflection of pressure on families—women are migrating as a means of reducing absolute dependence on agriculture. As jobs are becoming harder to secure, and as remittances thin out in many parts of western and southern Africa, many families are relying increasingly on women and their farming activities. As men increasingly migrated from rural areas, small holder agriculture became increasingly feminized. Women who are left behind are assuming new roles as resource mangers and decision makers, particularly within the agricultural sector.

Women face sexual harassment in the process of searching for employment, or because of their inability to secure it. Women face discrimination in securing accommodation in town, and stiff competition with men in employment, even after surviving discrimination in educational opportunities (Adepoju, 2003b). Women migration may also result in loss of rights to village lands. Some employers also exploit the vulnerable situation of newly-arrived female migrants desperate for a job. Those who migrate and are unemployed at destination may end up becoming sex workers and contract STIs, including HIV/AIDS; some may become single parents in the process, thus becoming a burden on their families.

REPRODUCTIVE HEALTH ISSUES IN THE CONTEXT OF THE MILLENNIUM DEVELOPMENT GOALS

Reproductive health is a state of complete physical, metal and social well-being in all maters relating to the reproductive system and to its functions and processes. It implies that people have the capability to reproduce and the freedom to decide if, when and how often to do so. Men and women need to have access to safe, effective, affordable and acceptable methods of family planning of their choice. Sexual health based on free choice also enhances life and personal relations (ICPD, 1994).

Since the 1994 International Conference on Population and Development, the paradigm shift from family planning to reproductive health has led to a considerable re-orientation of population programmes. Safe motherhood, ensuring maternal health and reducing maternal and infant mortality, became important components of reproductive health (IPPF, 1998). Other key elements include meeting the needs for family planning, preventing and treating sexually transmitted diseases—including HIV/AIDS—and eliminating traditional practices such as female genital cutting that are harmful to women's reproductive health and well-being. Many African countries now have in place comprehensive population policies and have updated them to incorporate the new orientations of the International Conference on Population and Development (ICPD) Programme of Action. In several countries, the revised policies recognize the importance of involving men more actively in planning and implementing population activities, in order to overcome resistance to family planning (Pietila, 2000).

Family planning, a major component of reproductive health (RH) in Africa, is designed to help couples and individuals: to prevent unwanted pregnancies and reduce the incidence of high-risk pregnancies, morbidity and mortality; to make quality services affordable, acceptable, and accessible to all who need and want them; to improve the quality of information, education, communication, counseling, and services; to increase the participation of men in the practice of family planning as well as their sharing of responsibility; and to promote breast-feeding to enhance birth spacing.

Africa is a region of high fertility, resulting from profound socio-cultural and economic factors: the early marriage of girls, the erosion of traditional long breast-feeding periods and post-partum sexual abstinence, poverty, the low status of women, illiteracy, and the limited use of effective contraceptives (Oppong, 1997). About 75 percent of girls in Africa aged 15 to 19 years become mothers, representing 13 percent of all fertility. Africa has the world's highest rate of births to very young mothers, about 40 percent to girls aged 17 years or under, compared to Latin America, Asia and Europe with 39, 31 and 22 percent, respectively (UNFPA, 1999). Africa's higher fertility rate reinforces poverty and deprivation and impacts negatively on the education, employment prospects and health of the young mothers and their children.

Africa today remains the only region that has not experienced a sustained transition to lower birth rates. Recent demographic and health surveys (DHS) show that, in spite of some commendable progress, few women of childbearing age in, for example, Senegal (7.4 percent in 1992/93) and Nigeria (12 percent in 1994) use modern contraceptives. In Kenya, Botswana and Zimbabwe, widespread female education and well-distributed health facilities, reinforced by strong political support, account for the relatively high contraceptive use of between 33 and 48 percent (Isiugo-Abanihe & Obono, 1999). The current economic crisis is also affecting the perceptions, orientation and behaviour of couples and families with respect to child-bearing. The very severe economic crisis, with its limited opportunities for employment, is forcing couples to delay marriage and to re-evaluate the value, cost and rewards of childbearing (Blanc and Poukouta, 1997). Widespread education also helps girls to postpone first birth, and promotes longer birth intervals as these young women opt for a small family size.

The dynamics described above are changing. Botswana and Zimbabwe are among the countries most infected by HIV/AIDS, with disastrous effects on infant mortality through transmissions from mothers to unborn children. Zimbabwe's economy is on the verge of collapse, inflation is at an all-time high, living conditions have plummeted and poverty is on the increase. Many couples who practise modern family planning methods probably begin doing so when the desired number of children have successfully survived infant and early adulthood mortality.

It is often assumed that Africa's women want fewer children because of the physiological effect childbearing has on their health and the burden of looking after many children. In the African patriarchal societies however, children, and especially sons, are valuable to women as a hedge against the risk of divorce, abandonment, widowhood, as well as for old age security (Mbugua, 1997). Hence greater structural changes are required, in both family-economy and national economies, and in the norms and values of family formation, to alter the habits that have encouraged large family size.

SAFE MOTHERHOOD

The status of women's reproductive health is still very poor in Africa and maternal mortality is one of the highest in the world, with thousands of women dying needlessly as a result of complications associated with pregnancy and childbirth.

The downturn in socio-economic conditions in Africa, deteriorating health and social facilities, poverty and an increasing inability of people to pay for health services has worsened maternal health status and the maternal mortality situation. As in most parts of the world, the major medical causes of maternal mortality are haemorrhage, obstructed labour, unsafe abortion, the hypertensive diseases of pregnancy, and sepsis. A large proportion of deliveries in the region takes place outside the supervision of skilled medical attendants (Alan Guttmacher Institute, 1995).

The declining but relatively high incidence of infant deaths still prompts mothers to have many children to ensure the survival of a few in the face of high infant mortality. Many women risk their health to have male children in competition with co-wives in polygynous marriages. Four groups of preventable diseases account for most childhood morbidity and mortality: malaria, diarrhoeal diseases, acute respiratory-tract infections and vaccine-preventable diseases. All of these are easily treated but continue to kill millions of African children yearly.

Women face a variety of health problems, including domestic violence, wife battery, incest and sexual abuse, and harmful cultural practices such as female genital cutting. In addition other negative cultural practices can be fostered by families: initiation rights for young girls, involving physical violation of their integrity and reproductive organs, continue in many societies while millions of young women suffer from vesicular vaginal fistula (VVF) as a result of early marriage, illiteracy, and poverty.

HARMFUL TRADITIONAL PRACTICES

Female genital cutting (FGC) is a leading harmful traditional practice injurious to the health of girls and women. It also exerts severe negative consequences on women's reproductive and mental health. This is purportedly done as a means of controlling promiscuity and women's sexual urges, and for preserving virginity before marriage and fidelity afterwards. Societies that practise FGC value female virginity highly; family honour and respect depend on a girl's ability to remain a virgin until the day of her marriage, and initiating a girl into womanhood is an intrinsic part of their cultural tradition. Because the external genitals are believed to be dirty, they are purportedly removed to promote hygiene and their aesthetic appeal to men (Coren, 2003). FGC is performed by traditional birth attendants, herbalists and elders using unsterilized knives, scalpel blades, pieces of glass and crude instruments without aseptic technique, thus exposing the girls and women to infection (Gilbert, 1993). The age of operation varies greatly; it could be done a few days after birth, during childhood, at the time of a woman's marriage—which could be before puberty—or at the birth of her first child (Momoh, 2003).

Several African countries—Somalia (where the practice is most widespread), Djibouti, Sudan, Ethiopia, Eritrea, Tanzania, Kenya, parts of DRC, Central African Republic, Mauritania, Benin, Burkina Faso, Cameroon, Chad, Côte d'Ivoire, Gambia, northern Ghana, Guinea, Guinea Bissau, Liberia, Mali, Niger, Senegal and Togo—practise FGC and, although it is outlawed in ten of these countries, enforcement is generally compromised (UNFPA, 1999). Apart from complications at delivery, FGC is also a potential route for the transmission of HIV/AIDS.

HIV/AIDS AND ITS SOCIO-DEMOGRAPHIC IMPACT

The HIV/AIDS pandemic is a major developmental challenge and is one of the most serious challenges to the wellbeing of African families today. Because of a variety of cultural and social practices, African families are being affected by HIV/AIDS in ways quite peculiar to the region where its transmission is almost universally heterosexual; infection through drug abuse, blood transfusion and homosexual contact is negligible. This means that everyone who is sexually active is at risk, as well as infants born to sero-positive mothers.

The Tunis Declaration on *AIDS and the Child in Africa*, adopted by the Heads of State and Government of the OAU in Tunis over a decade ago (13–15 June, 1994), painted the following gloomy picture: 'About 1 million infections occur annually in men, women and children; by the year 2000, about 20 million Africans will be infected with HIV'; adding that '…AIDS causes sickness and despair, kills young and middle-aged adults, who are parents, the mainstay of the family, the backbone of the workforce, and the care givers to our young; that children are infected by various modes of transmission and girls are particularly vulnerable to infection through sexual intercourse by adults.'

The grim facts of AIDS in Africa are a serious cause for concern. Africa accounts for the bulk of global infections which has orphaned over 11 million children in the region. Most Africans infected with HIV/AIDS live in absolute poverty, and most of the gains achieved up till now in life expectancy are now threatened by the pandemic, with profound economic and health consequences. The UNAIDS (2003) indicates that, out of 40 million people worldwide with HIV/AIDS, 30 million are in Africa. In 2003, 3.5 million new infections were reported, and approximately 2.5 million people died, bringing to more than 15 million the African victims of the epidemic since its appearance in the early 1980s. Ten million of those infected in Africa are believed to be young people aged 15–24 years, and three million are less than 15 years old. In the worst-affected countries, two in every five adults are infected; less than 1 percent of pregnant women receive the information and treatment needed to avoid passing HIV to their children, and only 2 percent of HIV-positive people who need treatment have access to it. These sobering figures reflect the many socio-economic consequences of the pandemic.

What distinguishes Africa from other parts of the world is that families are the centre of HIV/AIDS transmission. The disease takes an unusually heavy toll on members of the same family, not just of the same household. In southern and eastern Africa, where large numbers of AIDS cases have been reported, survivors of decimated families are usually grandfathers, grandmothers and grandchildren. In parts of Malawi, Zambia and Tanzania, an entire generation of fathers, mothers, aunts and uncles has been lost. Consequently, AIDS orphans are reared in difficult social contexts by surviving relatives who are themselves physically and financially handicapped and emotionally traumatized. Such orphans are likely to grow up deprived educationally, emotionally and financially, thus becoming a likely source of future delinquency. Already many African families have demonstrated their inability to handle family members suffering from AIDS, preferring instead to abandon them, and to disassociate themselves from kin members whom they suspect of having been exposed to the virus.

In Africa the impact of the infection is severe on families. In some sub-Saharan African countries, between 10 and 30 percent of pregnant women in some localities have been infected with the virus. About 50 percent of the children born of those mothers will be sero-positive, and half of them are likely to develop AIDS and die from it. AIDS is responsible for the presence of untold numbers of orphans, as both parents and especially male heads of households die from it. Beside the severe strains that AIDS is placing on the already overstretched public and clinical health services, the social aspects of its ravages have a devastating effect on families. Since health systems cannot cope with the variety and intensity of morbidity arising from HIV, the largest burden for dealing with it has been shifted to families. These have to undertake the long-term nursing of their stricken members and the care of orphans further draining their inadequate resources.

Several social and cultural behaviours common to Africa promote the spread of HIV/AIDS. Early age of first sexual contact exposes young people to HIV/AIDS for a longer period of their lives, raising the probability of contracting the disease. Marital dissolutions and the pressure to commercialize sex as economies continue to suffer, labour migration, which separates spouses, altering sex ratios and creating markets for prostitution, all facilitate the spread of AIDS. In many African societies, particularly in eastern and southern Africa, the practice of levirate can wipe out entire extended families if the spouse or spouses of the dead man are infected with HIV (Gaigbe-togbe and Meinberger, 2003). Despite campaigns to eradicate levirate, the practice has proved resistant to change as it is so closely linked to the rules of inheritance and the distribution and right to the wealth and property of the deceased.

The unwillingness of African men to use condoms and the practice of multiple partnerships are particularly favourable to HIV/AIDS transmission. While girlfriends and mistresses may be able to negotiate the use of a condom, the same does not apply to wives, leading to HIV/AIDS transmission among married women from their husbands. Less than a third of young people in the worst-affected countries use condoms with non-regular sexual partners.

HIV/AIDS and premature death among youths have brought in their trail a reversal of roles—the elderly may have to cater for their orphaned grandchildren since urbanization, migration and unemployment render those from who they would normally have expected support are today economically dependant. Yet there is no viable government intervention for the care of the elderly to complement dwindling family support.

CARE AND SUPPORT OF THE ELDERLY

Africa, like other regions, is experiencing a silent demographic phenomenon—that of population ageing. In traditional African societies, families are primarily responsible for supporting the elderly, a support normally provided with devoted dedication. The elderly were held in high esteem in cultural and traditional matters and in the traditional setting ample support for older people was guaranteed within closely knit, age-integrated societies (Apt, 2001). The processes of urbanization and modernization are currently accelerating the destabilization of traditional values and weakening the traditional kinship mode of residential settlement. This affects the elderly in a number of ways, not least of which involves spatial residential dislocation of members of the family and erratic support and care for the elderly.

The ability of families, the principal source of support for the elderly, has been stretched to the limit. Deteriorating economic conditions and widespread unemployment have constrained the capacity of active members of families to adequately perform their traditional role towards the elderly despite the absence of formal social services. Gratuity and pension schemes, where in force, cover only retirees from the public and some private sectors and, except in South Africa, only very few elderly benefit from the paltry sums, often paid in arrears. Even then these recipients, as much as those without pension, find it increasingly difficult to meet their basic health care needs (Noumbissi, 2003). The worsening financial situation of the elderly is now manifested in street begging and public alms solicitation, hitherto the exclusive realm of the invalid and handicapped (Togonu-Bikersteth et al, 1997).

The current economic crisis, social transformation, poverty and the erosion of their economic independence compound the challenges facing the elderly. More and more, elderly parents are relocating to join their children in the cities to assist with the upbringing and fostering of their grandchildren. This dislocation has an adverse effect on the social integration of the elderly, weakening kinship ties within extended families (Shuman, 1991). In urban areas, full-time employment reduces the disposable time devoted to the care of family members, especially the elderly. In such a setting, a series of coping mechanisms have evolved including placing old parents in institutional home care and hiring live-in carers for elderly parents. This is a departure from the traditional practice in extended families where several generations live together within the same compound, a co-residence pattern that facilitates inter-generational exchanges between the elderly and other family members and where wives, daughter-in-laws and female grandchildren shoulder the day-to-day responsibility for the elderly.

Women who survive their husbands are often discriminated against by family members of their late spouses and may be denied the support they need in their old age. In many societies, they cannot inherit the property of the deceased spouse, and are often neglected, dispossessed, rejected, isolated, abused and even accused of killing their spouses with witchcraft (Adepoju, 2003a; HelpAge, 2002).

Loneliness and abandonment, in particular among widows and widowers and the childless, and especially in rural areas, are traumatic experiences for the elderly. Childlessness can be traumatic at all times but care for childless persons in old age is culturally viewed with impatience. The elderly perceive growing old as a period characterized by hardship and misery, social ostracism, inadequate care, ill-health, weakness and being a burden on others. In rural areas, the elderly may be viewed as possessing strange supernatural powers which can cause misfortune in their community and so can be highly susceptible to accusations of witchcraft, being ostracized or stoned to death—as has happened in parts of Tanzania (HelpAge 2002). Their frail look and the cumulative effect of poverty compound their physical decline, often prompting rejection in society. In some communities in southern Africa, sexual abuse among the elderly population has increased, fuelled by the myth that sex with older people can cure AIDS.

Faced with dwindling household human and financial resources and the increasing cost of health care, the elderly are often the last to benefit from the scanty health care services. With deteriorating physical health and a diminished ability to work, the elderly find that illness poses a major threat. The situation is worsened by social exclusion, the diminishing of the safety nets of the extended family and the absence of social welfare schemes for the elderly (Unanka, 2002). Years of hard labour, poor nutrition, repeated child birth (multi-parity) and inadequate health facilities compound women's health status at old age.

How vulnerable, and resilient, are African families and its members—children, youths, men and women, and the elderly—in the face of these challenges?

6

Vulnerability and resilience of African families

The centrality of the African family

The Dakar/Ngor Declaration on Population, Family and Sustainable Development (1992) succinctly emphasized the centrality of the African family in reproduction, production and management of the environment and the successful implementation of population programmes in the region (UNECA, 1992). That was the African position at the 1994 International Conference on Population and Development (ICPD), a forum that considerably widened and deepened the global orientation of activities concerning population. However, a variety of factors—poor economic performance and mismanaged economies, failed states, political instability, conflicts, environmental disasters, the debt burden, poverty, and the excruciating social and economic effects of HIV/AIDS—have constrained the prospects of achieving the goals and targets set by various international conferences such as the ICPD Programme of Action 1994, the WSSD (World Summit for Social Development) Declaration and Programme of Action 1995, the FWCW (Fourth World Conference on Women) Platform for Action 1995 (United Nations, 1998). Consequently Africa's socio-economic and demographic indicators remain a serious concern.

As a way of redirecting attention to the persistence of the family as the most enduring and fundamental unit of society, the United Nations General Assembly proclaimed 1994 as the International Year of the Family (IYF). Activities related to the IYF were used to create greater awareness of the need to rethink strategies: to strengthen the family, to make it more efficient in its functions and to incorporate it as an integral institution of development planning (United Nations, 1991b). Ten years on, in spite of the daunting challenges and opportunities, African families do remain a dominant institution in society.

Families are vulnerable to crises. In general, families are sensitive to strains induced by social and economic changes. Families in difficult life situations, including the increasing numbers of vulnerable families—single-parent families headed by women, poor families with elderly members or those with disabilities, refugee and displaced families, and families with members affected by AIDS—require the special attention of governments and communities (ICPD, 1994). This is particularly the case because migration, poverty, forced population movements caused by conflicts and wars, and natural disasters have all strained to the limit the capacity of the extended families to support those who have traditionally depended on them.

The majority of African families have realized only a marginal improvement in their socio-economic positions as their quality of life and solidarity are challenged by high HIV/AIDS prevalence, by refugees and displaced persons flowing from civil and political conflicts competing for increasingly scarce resources, and by fast-growing populations and levels of urbanization. The rapid spread of HIV/AIDS is a major development challenge to African governments and families, all the more since the youth are the most heavily infected.

The other challenges that African families and society are contending with today are complex and are no less daunting. These include socio-economic disequilibrium marked by chronic unemployment, malnutrition, poverty and illiteracy, the debt burden, endemic conflicts, and economic deterioration. These have adversely affected the capacities of states to tackle key developmental problems such as illiteracy, lack of educational opportunities, inadequate institutional capacity, poor health infrastructure, poverty, unemployment, rural degradation and so on. Families are at the receiving end of the consequences of these interlocked crises.

Traditional African family values and practices are being challenged by external and internal dynamics. Traditional African values and practices promote childbearing throughout the reproductive span and the cultural attitudes and social practices favouring large families are deep-rooted. Fertility has always remained high in Africa, initially to compensate for the low survival rate of children, but also because of social and economic structures that of their nature sustain high fertility regimes. The obstacles to reductions in fertility in the region are enormous and complex. They include long-standing prejudices against the small family as a norm, low contraceptive use in the face of high infant mortality, high illiteracy, and male resistance to female contraception. In addition there is inadequate access to safe, affordable, effective and culturally acceptable modern methods of contraception, and lingering religious opposition to its use. For the African woman, couple and family, bearing a child has multifaceted advantages in spite of economic stress, education, new ideas generated by the western media and legislative measures which are producing changes in family norms and ideas.

Within the wide variety of political, economic and socio-cultural systems, the basic features of the marriage institution exhibit considerable common characteristics across the continent. The changes sweeping Africa today are in most areas transforming families, and include the co-existence of a wide range of different forms of marriage within the same society, socio-cultural group or nations. The general trend is toward the detachment of the extended family from the nuptial decision-making process, and a consequent increasing shift of the costs, responsibilities and decisions concerning marriage onto individuals—the prospective couples. Polygamy persists in many areas, even metamorphosing into practices such as the '*deuxieme bureaux*' ('second office') or 'outside wife'. At the same time, however, consensual and informal unions are becoming more prevalent and the ease with which people can get in and out of marriage without any fear of being socially or legally sanctioned is gradually undermining responsible parenthood and promoting the disintegration of Africa families. Modernization is undermining traditional family life and values while failing to replace these with new forms capable of meeting the needs once served by traditional practices (Mbugua, 1992).

Significant changes have been brought about in family forms and household composition through migration and urbanization. Labour migration has meant that women who have to provide for their children, often in the absence of regular remittances, head many households. Female labour migration has increased in recent years and women who migrate to urban areas often leave their children with their own mother, thus creating households without resident wage earners. High rates of divorce, increased parental conflict and the escalating costs of welfare programmes, coupled with rising crime, drug taking and anti-social behaviour among the young, are evidence that African families and their social values have been disrupted. In female-headed households, the problem of juvenile delinquency is fast becoming evident, particularly among boys who, in the absence of their fathers, rebel against the authority of their mothers.

Dysfunctional families are mushrooming. The dominant authority of the father, mother or both is gradually being eroded; social institutions are also being affected, bringing the family to a crisis point. The changes in the role and status of women and loss of power of the father have brought a great challenge to child parenting and management. Nevertheless, the primary role of parents in the personality and the developmental psychology of children remain very crucial, since unless the foundation laid by the parents is very sound, the child starts life at a great disadvantage and could later become a problem to self, parents and society as a whole.

Women are undergoing considerable stress in performing their varied roles. Women's multiple and complex roles—as wife, mother, housekeeper, household manager, worker, kinswoman and citizen, child-bearer and child-rearer, food producer and processor—create stress for women. African women combine reproductive and productive tasks and responsibilities within the family context. Their levels of both fertility and economic activity are higher than in other parts of the world. They are compelled to initiate both these activities at an earlier age than do women elsewhere and depend, to a greater extent, on support from kin in carrying out these heavy and frequently conflicting tasks. The multiplicity of roles for women under very stressful conditions calls for programmatic interventions for women, to enhance their skills, knowledge, opportunities for self-realization and support services.

Women in Africa continue to encounter gender-specific obstacles in various fields of national life; they are often discriminated against in employment, in economic opportunities and in access to credit, and are marginalized politically. Most programmes ostensibly set up to cater for women's welfare are constrained by high institutional budgets, with little allocated for grassroots' activities and for the health, education and income-generating opportunities of women. These programmes also lack continuity, visibility and sustainability.

Adolescents and youths are losing out on both formal and family life education. Education for their children is today out of reach for most women or families, with the consequence that growth in primary education has slowed down by as much as 50 per cent in many African countries. The high proportions of teenage pregnancies, and the increasing drop out rate among young girls, signal prospects for higher fertility as this large cohort enter into regular sexual activity at a very early age but have limited access to information and family planning services. Yet population policies for the youth tend to treat early sexual activity as an exception rather than as the rule. Family life education programmes are introduced so late in high schools that at least half of the recipients would already have been engag-

ing in sexual intercourse for three or four years, and the content is diluted to such an extent that it becomes ineffectual. Such programmes fail to equip the youth with the skills and knowledge on how to cope with their own turbulent emotions, STIs, problems associated with early pregnancies, contraception and the risks of abortion (Adepoju, Adunola, 2005).

Family hierarchies are being challenged as women take on new roles and family members enter waged employment, and state institutions are displacing the family's central authoritative role. Family solidarity and the control once exerted by the family as a group are both weakening, as changes take place in a range of institutions central to the family and family law—changes in marriage customs, bride-wealth, maintenance of dependants and inheritance. This trend should be reversed.

Economic restructuring programmes are impoverishing and impacting negatively on the health of African family members. 'Structural adjustment' programmes (SAPs) have impacted severely on African families in the sectors of education, health and employment. SAP 'reform' measures are mainly short-term and do not address long-term concerns of structural transformation, sustained economic growth and sustainable development. To conform to structural adjustment conditionality, governments removed subsidies on health and education, calling for parents to pay the cost of health and education services. A large proportion of heads of families—jobless parents—were unable to pay the higher costs of these services, and have had to withdraw their children and wards from school as well as having to opt for traditional or religious forms of healing. This practice impacts negatively on child survival and the general health conditions of the vulnerable poor, including children and the elderly. Increasingly, countries are being forced to jettison some of the traditional components of population policies and programmes.

Poverty is widespread and impacts on family welfare. Poverty, though widespread, is most concentrated among the unemployed and underemployed youths, small farm households, and households headed by informal-sector workers, women or elderly persons without social safety nets. Poverty is a state of deprivation through lack of access to economic and social resources and is manifested in illiteracy, lack of access to water, poor housing and declining purchasing power. Low education levels, poor health, poor nutrition, low incomes, large family size, and food insecurity are among the factors that contribute to poverty at the micro level of the family. For about half of African families, poverty is so widespread

and deep-rooted that access to adequate food, clean water, safe sanitation, reliable health care, decent housing and a basic education constitutes a vital dream, but one yet to be achieved.

The debt overhang constrains efforts of governments and families to improve living conditions. Devoting their limited resources to repaying external debts deprives African countries of the ability to solve a series of socio-economic problems confronting African families.[1] Efforts by several countries to restructure their economies, privatize state-controlled entities, devalue their currencies, and open their markets to share in the global economy have been disappointing. Today most youths are still illiterate, unemployed, disillusioned and at risk of HIV/AIDS infection. Ethnic conflicts that create incessant refugee flows, displace populations, and stall efforts to eradicate poverty, are likely to increase. Distressful economic and living conditions continue to trigger the emigration of men and women professionals.

Farm productivity has steadily declined and food security has been jeopardized in areas where large numbers of people, especially men, have migrated for long periods. Collateral requirements, based on land or property ownership, can accentuate poverty for women who seldom hold title to such assets. Women farmers and women left behind are seriously affected as lack of title to land can block their access to agricultural credit, services, and aids. In addition, women farmers rarely have direct contact with agricultural extension agents, and even when they are reached, their limited education may prevent these women from using agricultural information effectively. Migration has nevertheless made it possible for single and unaccompanied married women to live and work in towns. Some of them, just like their male counterparts, send money home to support their aged parents and pay school fees for their relatives. They also make substantial contributions towards developmental projects.

The HIV/AIDS epidemic compounds other problems faced by families. The death of parents often results in the break-up of households, with children being fostered by relatives or becoming homeless. The loss of the agricultural labour force in the worst-affected countries has grave consequences for family food secu-

---

1.   The recent announcement by the G8 countries to write off the debts of 18 heavily indebted countries, 14 of which are in Africa, is a welcome development, the more so since it was made on condition that these countries utilize these funds judiciously for improving education, health and related infrastructures.

rity. Households affected by HIV/AIDS often withdraw children from school to help at home with care-giving or income-generating activities (UNAIDS, 2003).

The HIV/AIDS epidemic has aggravated the problems faced by the elderly. With children who traditionally provide economic security for the aged infected by HIV, parents are burdened with expensive care and treatment. Upon their parents' death, orphaned children must be cared for by ageing grandparents. Lacking knowledge of the disease, the elderly are exposed to infection and the destruction of their household security. Yet HIV/AIDS awareness campaigns generally ignore the elderly even though they are often susceptible to the risk of contracting it (HelpAge, 2002).

7

Overview and the way forward

In spite of the pressures brought to bear on them, African families have not disintegrated; rather their roles and structure have undergone dramatic changes in response to the economic crisis, environmental deterioration and rapid growth of the population. Their resilience is anchored in the norms, values, practices and beliefs that sustain it from one crisis to another. These crises have perhaps reinforced the African family's resilience to withstand the onslaught of westernizing, urbanization, globalization, the Internet, and an unprecedented multimedia blitz. *Such a steadfast unit is clearly worthy and deserving of more attention than has been accorded to it thus far.*

African governments and development partners need to recognize the centrality of the family as the focal point of any people-centred development. Past attempts to compartmentalize families into different target groups for each sector have yielded poor results because such paradigms have been, and continue to be, at best inappropriate and at worst irrelevant.

Traditional systems for controlling, monitoring, protecting and supporting both the young and the elderly are breaking down in the context of economic crisis. This is exacerbated by spatial dislocations of people seeking new sources of security and support. The consequences affect areas such as the socialization of young people, sexual relations, fertility management, and parental responsibility. *Policy measures should programme interventions creatively to support the economic situation of families—for instance by introducing subsidies for vulnerable and poor families—to enable them perform their traditional roles more effectively.*

Employment opportunities should be created for young people. Structural adjustment programmes have led to rising illiteracy as families withdraw children, especially girls, from school. As African governments continue to restructure their economies, the burden of cost recovery is increasingly being shifted to families.

Educational reforms must provide life-long functional literacy for young people, and make them employable in the rapidly competitive, globalizing labour market.

African governments will need to design appropriate development paradigms to help generate viable employment opportunities for the teeming youth population and to help cushion the negative effects on families of education cost recovery programmes. It is only in this way that youths can be empowered to use their latent energies for productive activities in economic, social, political and community activities and prepare themselves adequately for their future parental responsibilities as well as behaving in a sexually responsible manner. Such measures could also help to reduce the increasing incidence of trafficking, drug abuse and violence among mostly unemployed youths.

Female education has cumulative effects on family welfare. African governments must pay more attention to raising female literacy as an end in itself but also because it has profound effects on the health and nutritional status of families and children. It has been demonstrated that the combined effects of female literacy, health and nutrition do in fact reduce infant mortality, reduce the prevailing high fertility and enhance the general health of families. Improvement in education for girl children could in the long run help improve family health, enhance their chances in the marriage market, reduce family size, increase opportunities for employment and enhance productivity, even in informal economic activities. The complex role of women can also be improved through education which empowers them to better realize their potentials.

Governments should eliminate gender discrimination in programme activities, empower women, build equality into all forms of human resource development and ensure that policies and programmes adopt gender perspectives in development planning. Appropriate mechanisms should be institutionalized to construct indicators of poverty as perceived by women to help in formulating policies that address their specific concerns.

To help increase women's productivity and earnings, agricultural and management training and skills development, access to credit and marketing programmes should be among interventions that target their specific needs. Direct assistance to women's agricultural and small businesses and a complete review of punitive regulations for informal small enterprises could help alleviate the poverty that has pushed many female migrants from their place of origin.

Poverty reduction strategies should be centred on families. The incidence, depth and severity of poverty in Africa today are such that poverty reduction strategies should be synonymous with economic growth and development strategies. The responsibility for fighting poverty should be borne by the government in partnership with communities and families at the grassroots level. In view of the demographic aspects of poverty, durable solutions for alleviating poverty should focus on households and families rather than on individuals. African governments' efforts to reduce poverty, and to improve the standard of living of individuals and families must constitute the corner-stone of a human-centred development strategy firmly anchored on the concept of the centrality of the family. *The promotion of smaller families, healthier, better-educated children who are better equipped to earn a living, must constitute integrated elements of such strategies.*

Poverty alleviation should be a continuous process of interventions, aimed primarily at improving the quality of life of poor people in general and poor women in particular. Planners should target development activities and programmes to reflect women's concerns, empower and give them access to and control of resources. Unemployment is a key factor in poverty, and ill-health perpetuates poverty. One way forward is to put in place appropriate measures to improve education and access to employment opportunities.

There is a significant impact on African families due to the demographic changes that have been occurring in a context of economic stagnation, recurrent crisis, spiralling debt burdens and the introduction, under international pressure, of structural adjustment programmes. The consequences of such programmes—falling living standards, unemployment, malnutrition, and reductions in public services—fall most heavily upon women. *Policies aimed at restructuring the economy, based largely upon family-run agricultural units and other micro-enterprises should be squarely based on the nature of the underlying family system.*

In view of SAPs' pervasiveness and generally negative impact in Africa, its linkages to demographic change at the micro-level of the individual and families (births, deaths, migratory movements) should be comprehensively addressed. This assessment needs to include the types of SAP-induced decisions that families are taking and their repercussions on the quality of their lives. Cushioning the effects of cost-recovery strategies on the health sector especially with respect to infant and child mortality and declining rates of educational enrolment, can help invigorate on-going development programmes.

Street children constitute a growing urban tragedy and are the products of poverty, famine, conflicts, migration, unemployment, and broken homes. The impact of these transformations on the social structure has been daunting and should be addressed comprehensively.

An understanding of reproduction in Africa calls for a systematic analysis of the institutions, norms, socio-economic structures, decision-making processes and value systems (at macro, meso and micro levels) which fostered and still sustain the high fertility norm at household level. African governments must continue to tackle vigorously the enormous obstacles to fertility reduction: as long as fertility remains high, families will continue to remain poor.

Low levels of contraceptive prevalence, coupled with the still-continuing demand for large families, implies a doubling of effort in making reproductive health services, including family planning, available, affordable and accessible. Reproductive health programme managers, including family planning managers, must be creative in packaging information, education and communication messages and in providing services innovatively through communities as well as through fully integrated family health care delivery systems. The 'unmet' gap should be bridged through a cost-effective method mix that is both culturally acceptable and effective.

Laws and legal provisions pertaining to the accessibility of family planning supplies and services in Africa are often cumbersome and are based on marital status rather than on exposure to sexual activity and should be reviewed. In Kenya, where a married teenage girl can access contraceptives of her own choice, she is legally denied such services if she divorces before she attains the age of majority, even if she has children (Mbugua, 1997). Abortion is prohibited altogether in most African countries except where the mother's life is in danger.

The role of men

Population programmes should also target men as key players, not only in procreation as customary heads of the family but also in decision-making regarding childbearing, as well as the adoption of small family size, and family planning in general. The effective participation of men in reproductive health, including family planning, should be promoted and sustained. It is also important to incorporate the consequences of HIV/AIDS in family planning and reproductive health programmes.

The role of parents and faith-based organisations

Parents, teachers, faith-based organizations, guardians, schools and society at large should complement advocacy programmes and population education for in-school children and at out-of-school posts, in order to re-inculcate the discipline, propriety and cultural values embodied in Africa's tradition with respect to the integrity of the family and responsible childbearing and childrearing norms. In particular, faith-based organizations should impart moral education to adolescents in order to fill the gaps which schools and families have failed to bridge.

Improved communication between parents and adolescents on sexuality and reproductive health matters is imperative. Adolescent pregnancies are now pervasive in societies that had strong traditional sanctions against pre-marital childbearing. In spite of the reality of the unmet needs of the youth, most population policies and programmes in Africa are still adamantly against the provision of contraceptive information and supplies to young people. Adolescents want their parents to be listeners, friends and counsellors: they feel alienated and abandoned by busy parents and, as an alternative, turn to their peers—who are equally poorly informed—for information on sexual and reproductive health issues.

The role of governmental and other organizations

The AIDS scourge has devastated African families in terms of disrupting the family-building process, generating untold numbers of widows, widowers and orphans, and straining health systems. *Educational campaigns and innovative programme responses to the effects of AIDS should be put in high gear. Concurrently communities should strive to forsake all traditional practices and norms that are implicated in the spread of HIV/AIDS.*

Since customs, values and morals do not die once, sustained advocacy is required to raise public awareness and change public opinion in favour of the total eradication of female genital cutting (FGC). Local level organizations can best address the specific cultural issues that sustain this practice. Training and retraining of practitioners is essential to limit and ultimately to eradicate FGC. While the practice lasts, its practitioners must provide ways of sterilizing their equipment to avoid infections like HIV. Those who have performed FGC as a profession should also, ideally, be provided with alternative means of livelihood.

Insightful research is required to deepen our understanding of the roles and constraints women face with respect to participation in development, access to and control of land, labour and production activities. The position of women in migration decision-making and in the control of resources should be critically evaluated, as should the influence of culture and religion on female migration, a process that is likely to become larger rather than smaller in the future.

In view of social disruptions and civil wars in several African countries, specific programmes need to be put in place to satisfy the nutritional requirements of children and to enhance the reproductive health of their mothers, who are the real victims of conflicts, disruptive population displacements and grinding poverty. The underlying factors that give rise to refugee flows and disruptive population displacements must be promptly and comprehensively addressed. Achieving sustainable livelihoods, food security, peace and stability is essential not only for sustainable development but crucially for the cohesion and survival of families in the region.

Globalization has impacted on adolescents' mode of dressing and this is evidenced by the scanty dressing of girls. A cultural awareness campaign should be mounted to educate adolescents, especially girls, to dress in a modern but dignified manner.

Governments should set up regulatory authorities to vet the barrage of pornographic materials, X-rated films and related materials in order to protect families, especially vulnerable young children from the onslaught of the powerful but unwholesome media blitz, the Internet and imported films, which could destroy African cultural values.

African governments should firmly recognize that the youth constitute the region's most viable resource and will, over the next few years, constitute a larger proportion of the total. Currently, a high proportion of the youth are mothers and fathers, and need adequate preparation for their responsibilities as parents. Parents should press for school biology curricula to contain elements of human reproduction at the higher levels of primary and the lower levels of secondary school, followed at subsequent levels by aspects of sexuality and adolescent reproductive health, and instructions on moral education for all.

Regarding the elderly, communities should initiate programmes that incorporate their well-being and include their active participation in community development in order to enhance their living conditions. Elements of such programmes should include small credit schemes to alleviate poverty, providing access to loans for small scale agricultural, trading and manufacturing enterprises, training of some of the elderly to become 'community gerontologists' and providing holistic care services for low-income older people. Also needed are the provision of out-reach services through mobile clinics for older and disabled persons and home visits to provide emotional and social support for the elderly. Families must strive to re-integrate the elderly and preserve the values traditionally placed on them.

Insightful research on the family should be promoted; current information is required for targeting programmes that address the needs of families and their members. Such research should focus simultaneously on the individual, the household, the community, and societal-level issues, in order to enhance our understanding of the socio-cultural and demographic factors associated with African families and hence for designing appropriate policy measures.

8

Conclusion

The review of the challenges facing African families in the new millennium firmly indicates that the family is the basic unit of society and remains an enduring institution in Africa. Marriage is the threshold to family formation, and families maintain varying measures of solidarity among their members through the institution of marriage, for instance through early marriage, mate selection and the payment of dowry. Childbearing is a fundamental aspect of family life that is rooted in African tradition, culture, and religion. High fertility permeates the fabric of African society and is sustained by early and often prolonged childbearing. Care of children is shared by members of the extended family and child fostering is a common practice. The African woman's multiple roles as daughter, wife, mother, housekeeper, worker, kinswoman and citizen are being reshaped by education, employment, current economic conditions, and migration.

African families are undergoing rapid transformation as a result of social change, modernization, globalization, poverty, conflicts and economic crisis. The most obvious changes experienced by African families are structural changes, reflected in a variety of forms of family and household which are emerging as are new marriage forms: single-, child-, female- and grandparent-headed, even 'skip' households. The typical nuclear family is a rare phenomenon in Africa.

The crises confronting African families and their members—children, adolescents and youths in particular—are numerous and daunting. Child labour is widespread in Africa as a result of generalized poverty and economic crisis. Street children as beggars are increasing in number in major cities, are vulnerable to exploitation and are easily drawn into prostitution, drug-taking, alcohol dependency and crime. Products of famine, armed conflicts, rural-urban migration, unemployment, poverty and broken families, such children constitute a growing urban tragedy.

Africa's adolescents and youths are sandwiched between the family and the state, between tradition and modernity and are inadequately prepared for the transition from childhood to youth and much less aware of their responsibilities as parents than previous generations were. Poverty, unemployment and weakening family control drive some youths to illicit activities; some fall prey to traffickers' rackets in a desperate search for survival. Thus, trafficking in illegal migrants, hitherto a rare phenomenon, is on the increase as young persons become involved in dare-devil ventures to gain entry into Europe. This development is traumatic, and reflects the depth of the deterioration of African economies, the extent of poverty and the desperation to survive.

Globalization, conflict and war, poverty and economic restructuring, rapid population growth, urbanization and migration, reproductive health, HIV/AIDS and harmful traditional practices, ageing, the care and support of the elderly are among the key challenges confronting African families today.

During the last two decades, Africa was indeed the most conflict-affected region in the world. These conflicts have had a profound impact on families with far-reaching effects on their solidarity and functions even as family fortunes have been wiped out. The acclimatization of youths to violence is a grave cause for concern. Woman abducted during periods of conflict and the children born to them are being rehabilitated by families or relatives from their meagre resources. The conscription of children as child-soldiers in the theatres of war in Africa is commonplace. Often the product of violence themselves and having witnessed the violent death of one or both parents, or of siblings and other kin members, they have grown up feeling rejected and alienated and, with no family ties or support, have turned to violence, drugs and delinquency.

War and internal conflicts and environmental disasters also generate millions of refugees and displaced persons in Africa and have severely affected local economies, families and people's lives. In the process of flight, families lose all or most of their belongings, property and land. Africa's refugee situation has been and remains a human tragedy in magnitude and complexity. As armed conflicts intensify, children, women and the elderly are the main victims, and the loss of the extended family as a traditional base for the care of the disabled, old people and orphans results in trauma and rejection for the affected people. Also the reproductive health of refugees and displaced persons is not always adequately and promptly addressed.

Most conflicts in Africa result from poverty, lack of respect for human rights, bad governance, corruption, and struggle for control of centrally dominated national resources. Globalization, some argue, can open a window of opportunity by linking local to international markets and generating employment. Even though Africa is marginalized in the global market, globalization has exposed many African countries to global risks and uncertainties, thereby increasing their vulnerability. Globalization is undermining Africa's human development, and families are at the receiving end of these changing configurations.

The disadvantageous position of African countries in the global era impacts on families in various ways. Agricultural subsidies in rich countries impoverish African farmers, forcing them to migrate to the cities—to what turns out to be only unemployment and misery. Restrictions on migration to developed countries foster illegal migration and curtail the potential for remittances. 'Western' media promotions are at variance with traditional values and norms of African families.

Poverty is pervasive in Africa and is at the root of many problems confronting African families today. In many African countries, the already poor social conditions of families are rendered poorer by so-called stabilization and adjustment measures. Access to education, health and other social services has been curtailed, thus reducing the overall welfare of families. The tremendous increase in women's work has seriously compromised their ability to perform their traditional family welfare and nurturing roles, has impoverished many women and perpetuated the intergenerational cycle of poverty.

Residential patterns of African families have changed in response to education, urbanization and migration. Migration has led to the emergence of dual households for many African families. Migration in Africa remains very much a 'family matter', and a variety of customs restricts female migration, as do job segregation and discrimination in the urban labour market. Two decades of economic distress and changing economic circumstances are however forcing communities to condone female migration. A significant proportion of educated women, single and married alike, now migrate alone to developed countries in search of greener pastures, leaving their children in the care of their husbands—an important reversal of traditional gender roles. Women may face sexual harassment in the process of searching for employment, or because of their inability to secure work. Some employers exploit the vulnerable situation of newly-arrived female migrants desperate for a job. Those unemployed at destination may end up becoming sex workers and contract sexually transmitted infections, including HIV/AIDS; some may become single parents in the process, thus putting an additional burden on their families.

The status of women's reproductive health is still very poor in Africa and maternal mortality is one of the highest in the world, with thousands of women dying annually as a result of complications associated with pregnancy and childbirth. This situation has been aggravated by the downturn in socio-economic conditions in the last decade, as well as by deteriorating health and social facilities, poverty and people's increasing inability to pay for health services. Women face a variety of serious health problems which impact on their reproductive health.

The HIV/AIDS pandemic is a major developmental challenge and is one of the most serious threats to the wellbeing of African families today. As the result of a variety of cultural and social practices, African families are being affected by HIV/AIDS in ways quite peculiar to the region where its transmission is almost universally heterosexual. Most Africans infected with HIV/AIDS live in absolute poverty. But what distinguishes Africa from other parts of the world is that the family is the centre of transmission, with the disease taking a heavy toll on members of the same family. Since health systems cannot cope with the variety and intensity of morbidity arising from HIV, the largest burden for dealing with it has been shifted to the families, further draining their inadequate resources.

Africa, like other regions, is experiencing a silent demographic phenomenon—that of population ageing. The ability of families to support their elderly has been stretched to the limit by the current economic crisis, as well as by social transformation and poverty. Illness poses a major threat at old age, a situation worsened by social exclusion, diminished safety nets of the extended family and absence of social welfare schemes for the elderly.

How vulnerable, and resilient, are African families in the face of the challenges to its members, straining to the limit their capacity for giving support? The majority of African families have realized only a marginal improvement in their socio-economic positions even as their quality of life is challenged by high HIV/AIDS prevalence, by refugees and displaced people fleeing from endemic civil and political conflicts, and by rapidly growing populations and urbanization, unemployment, malnutrition, poverty and illiteracy, by the debt burden and by general economic deterioration. Dysfunctional families are mushrooming: The dominant authority of parents is gradually being eroded and adolescents and youths are losing out on formal family life education.

Economic restructuring under the tenets of structural adjustment programmes are impoverishing and impacting negatively on the health of African family members, constraining access to education, health and employment. Poverty is widespread and impacts on family welfare. The debt overhang constrains efforts of governments and families to improve living conditions as resources devoted to repaying external debts deprive African countries of the ability to solve the socio-economic problems confronting African families. Food security is threatened by a steady decline in farm productivity in HIV/AIDS affected areas, as well as in localities where large numbers of men have migrated for survival for long periods. Migration is also eroding day-to-day mutual support among family members.

The following recommendations are aimed at strengthening the institution of the family, Africa's enduring and multifunctional unit. A resilient institution, the African family has not disintegrated, in spite of the pressures brought to bear on it.

- African governments and their development partners should recognize the centrality of the family. Efforts to reduce poverty, improve the standard of living of individuals and families must constitute the corner-stone of a human-centred development strategy firmly anchored on the concept of the centrality of the family. Policy measures should creatively programme interventions to reinforce the economic situation of families, for instance by introducing subsidies for vulnerable and poor families, thus enabling their members to perform their traditional roles more effectively.

- Educational reforms must provide life-long functional literacy for young people, and make them employable in the competitive, globalizing labour market. African governments will need to (re)design appropriate development paradigms to help generate viable employment opportunities for the teeming youth population. The main route to exit poverty is gainful employment.

- Female education has cumulative effects on family welfare: African governments must pay more attention to raising female literacy, both as an end in itself and also because it has profound effects on the health and nutritional status of families. Governments should eliminate gender discrimination in programme activities, empower women and build equality into all forms of human resource development.

- Insightful research is required to deepen our understanding of the roles and constraints women face with respect to participation in development, access to and control of land, as well as in labour and production activities.

- Because of the pervasiveness and generally negative impact of structural adjustment programmes (SAPs) in Africa, there is a need to address comprehensively the linkages of SAPs to demographic change at the micro-level of the individual and the family.

- The promotion of smaller families, and healthier, better-educated children, equipped to earn a living must constitute integrated elements of development strategies.

- Policies that include a focus on family-run agricultural units and other micro-enterprises, and are aimed at restructuring the economy, should be squarely based on the nature of the underlying family systems.

- Street children constitute a growing urban tragedy, being the products of poverty, famine, conflicts, migration, unemployment, and broken homes. The impact of transformations on urban social structure must be addressed comprehensively.

- Reproductive health programme managers must be creative in providing information and services innovatively through communities as well as through fully-integrated family health care delivery systems.

- The effective participation of men in reproductive health programmes, including family planning, should be promoted and sustained. It is also important to incorporate the consequences of HIV/AIDS in family planning.

- Parents, guardians, teachers, schools and society at large should complement advocacy programmes and population education for in-school children and out-of-school adolescents and youths. Faith-based organizations can also help by imparting further moral education to young people. A cultural awareness campaign should be mounted to educate young persons, especially girls, on dress codes that are modern yet dignified.

- Communication between parents and adolescents on sexuality and reproductive health matters should be improved: young people need appropriate information on the transmission, prevention and impact of HIV/AIDS. Educational campaigns by religious, traditional and community leaders and innovative programme responses to AIDS should be put in high gear.

- The underlying factors that give rise to refugee flows and disruptive population displacements must be promptly and comprehensively addressed. Achieving sustainable livelihoods, food security, peace and stability, is essential not only for sustainable development but crucially for the cohesion and survival of families in the region. Specific programmes should be put in place to enhance the nutritional requirements and reproductive health of children and their mothers, who are the real victims of conflicts, disruptive population displacements and grinding poverty.

- Governments that have not yet done so should set up regulatory authorities to vet pornographic material since these could help destroy African cultural values.

- Communities should initiate programmes that incorporate the well-being and active participation of the elderly in community development in order to enhance their living conditions.

- Research as a basis for designing appropriate policy measures on the family should focus simultaneously on individual, household, community and societal-level factors.

Above all, policies in the economic, social, demographic and political spheres should be anchored on the needs, potentialities and constraints of African families and by the gender of its component members—children, adolescents, youths, adults and the elderly. It is in this way that the millennium development goals of eradicating extreme poverty, improving nutrition and productivity, enhancing food security and living conditions, reducing child mortality and improving maternal health, promoting gender equality in access to education and combating HIV/AIDS, malaria and other diseases that plague the continent can be achieved.

References

Abdellaziz, B.H. 2003. The concept of globalization: framework for Africa's response on 'strategies for making globalization work for all'. Paper presented at the *Fourth African Population Conference*. Tunis, 8–12 December: Union for African Population Studies.

Adekanye, J. Bayo. 1998. Conflicts, Loss of State Capacities and Migration in Contemporary Africa. In R. Appleyard (ed.), *Emigration Dynamics in Developing Countries: Vol. 1: Sub-Saharan Africa*. Aldershot: Ashgate.

Adepoju, Aderanti. 1977. Rationality and Fertility in the Traditional Yoruba Society, South-West Nigeria. In J.C. Caldwell (ed.), *The Persistence of High Fertility: Population Prospects in The Third World. Vol 1*. Canberra: Australian National University Press.

Adepoju, Aderanti. 1989. The consequences of the influx of refugees for countries of asylum in Africa. In R. Appleyard (ed.), *The Impact of International Migration on Developing Countries*. Paris: Organization for Economic Co-operation and Development.

Adepoju, Aderanti. 1990. State of the art review of migration in Africa. In *The Role of Migration in African Development: Issues and Policies for the 90s, UAPS Commissioned Papers*. Dakar: Union for African Population Studies.

Adepoju, Aderanti. 1995. Emigration dynamics in Sub-Saharan Africa. *International Migration* Vol. 33, Nos. 3 & 4.

Adepoju, Aderanti. 1996. *Population, Poverty, Structural Adjustment Programmes and Quality of Life in Sub-Saharan Africa*. Dakar: PHRDA.

Adepoju, Aderanti. 1997 (ed.). *Family, Population and Development in Africa*. London & New Jersey: Zed Books Ltd.

Adepoju, Aderanti. 2001. Population and Sustainable Development in Africa in the 21st Century: Challenges and Prospects. *HRDC African Policy Research Series No. 1*. Lagos: Concept Publications.

Adepoju, Aderanti. 2003a. Dynamics of Ageing and Support of the Elderly in Nigeria. *HRDC Policy Paper No 2*. Lagos: Concept Publications.

Adepoju, Aderanti. 2003b. Feminisation of poverty: perspectives from women in Nigeria's urban centres. *HRDC Research Series No. 4*. Lagos: Concept Publications.

Adepoju, Aderanti. 2003c. Continuity and changing configurations of migration to and from the Republic of South Africa. *International Migration* Vol. 41, No. 1.

Adepoju, Aderanti. 2005. Review of Research Data on Trafficking in Sub-Saharan Africa. *International Migration* Vol. 43, Nos.1& 2.

Adepoju, Adunola. 2001. *Perspectives on Population Education in Nigeria*, Lagos: Concept Publications.

Adepoju, Adunola. 2005. *Sexuality and Life Skills Education*. London: PenPress Publishers.

Aderinto, A.A. 2003. Socio-economic profiles, reproductive health behaviour and problems of street children in Ibadan, Nigeria. Paper presented at the *Fourth African Population Conference*. Tunis, 8–12 December: Union for African Population Studies.

Alan Guttmacher Institute. 1995. *Hopes and Realities; Closing the gap between women's aspirations and their reproductive experiences*. New York: Alan Guttmacher Institute.

Amin, S. 1974. Introduction, in Amin, S. (ed.) *Modern Migrations in Western Africa*. London: Oxford University Press.

Apt, N.A. 2001. Rapid Urbanization and Living Arrangements of Older Persons in Africa. *Population Bulletin of the United Nations Vol.* 42 & 43.

Armstrong, A. 1997. Law and the family in Southern Africa. In A. Adepoju (ed.), *Family, Population and Development in Africa*. London & New Jersey: Zed Books Ltd.

Blanc, A.K. & Poukouta, P.V. 1997. Components of unexpected fertility decline in sub-Saharan Africa. *Demographic Health Survey, Analytical Reports No. 5.* DHS, Calverton, MD, USA: Macro International Inc.

Blavo, E.Q. 1999. *The Problems of Refugees in Africa*. Aldershot: Ashgate.

Buchan, J. and Dovlo, D. 2004. *International recruitment of health workers in the UK: A report for DFID*. London: DFID Health Systems Resource Centre.

Campbell, E.K. & Ntsabane, T. 1995. *Street Children in Gaborone, Botswana: Causes and Policy Implications. UAPS Research Report*. Dakar: Union for African Population Studies.

Chojnacka, H. 2000. Early marriage and polygyny: feature characteristics of nuptiality in Africa. *Genus* Vol. 56, Nos. 3 & 4.

Colleta, N.J. et al. 1996. *The Transition from War to Peace in sub-Saharan Africa*. Washington, DC: The World Bank.

Coren C. 2003. Genital cutting may alter, rather than eliminate, women's sexual sensations. *International Family Planning Perspectives* Vol. 29, No. 1.

Crisp, J. 2000. Africa's Refugees: Patterns, Problems and Policy Challenges. *Journal of Contemporary African Studies* Vol. 18, No. 2.

Findley, S. 1997. Migration and family interactions in Africa. In A. Adepoju (ed.), *Family, Population and Development in Africa*. London and New Jersey: Zed Books Ltd.

FWCW (Fourth World Conference on Women). *1995. Platform for Action*. Beijing: Fourth World Conference on Women.

Gaigbe-togbe, V. & Weinberger M. 2003. The Social and economic implications of HIV/AIDS. Paper presented at the *Fourth African Population Conference*. Tunis, 8–12 December: Union for African Population Studies.

Gilbert, D. 1993. For the sake of purity (and control). Female genital mutilation. *LINKS. Health and Development Report* Vol. 9, No. 5.

HelpAge International. 2002. *State of the World's Older People 2002*. London: HelpAge International.

Human Rights Watch. 2003. *Borderline Slavery: Child Trafficking in Togo*, Vol. 15, No. 8(A).

ICPD (International Conference on Population and Development) with United Nations. 1994. Programme of Action adopted at the *International Conference on Population and Development*, Cairo, 5–13 September, 1994

ILO (International Labour Organization). 2003. *Trafficking in Human Beings: New Approaches to Combating the Problem: Special Action Programme to Combat Forced Labour*. ILO: Geneva.

IPPF (International Planned Parenthood Federation). 1998. *Planned Parenthood Challenges 1998 Vol. 1: Safe Motherhood*. London: International Planned Parenthood Federation.

Isiugo-Abanihe, U.C. 1985. Child fosterage in West Africa. *Population and Development Review* Vol. 11, No. 1.

Isiugo-Abanihe, U.I. & Obono M.O. 1999. Family Structure in sub-Saharan Africa: Tradition and Transition. In *Third African Population Conference: The African Population in the 21ˢᵗ Century Vol. 3*. Durban: UAPS/NPU.

Kibreab, G. 1983. Reflections on the African Refugee Problem: A Critical Analysis of Some Basic Assumptions. *Scandinavian Institute of African Studies, Research Report No. 67*. Uppsala: The Scandinavian Institute of African Studies.

Leidenfrost, N.B. (ed.). 1992. *Families in Transition: 1994 International Year of the Family*. Vienna: International Federation for Home Economics.

Locoh, T. 1988. The Evolution of the Family in Africa. In E. Van de Walle, et al (eds.), *The State of African Demography*. Liege: IUSSP.

Makinwa-Adebusoye, P. K. 1990. Female migration in Africa: an overview. In *The Role of Migration in African Development: Issues and Policies for the 90s. UAPS Commissioned Papers*. Dakar: Union for African Population Studies.

Makinwa-Adebusoye, P. K. 1997. The African family in rural and agricultural activities. In Adepoju, Aderanti (ed.) *Family, Population and Development in Africa*. London & New Jersey: Zed Books Ltd.

Martin, S.B. 1991. *Refugee Women*. London and New Jersey: Zed Books Ltd.

Mbugua, W. 1992. The dynamics and structure of family formation in Africa; a review and synthesis of current evidence. In *The Structure and Dynamics of Family Formation in Africa*. Dakar: Union for African Population Studies.

Mbugua, W. 1997. The African family and the status of women's health. In A. Adepoju (ed.), *Family, Population and Development in Africa*. London & New Jersey: Zed Books Ltd.

Momoh, C. 2003. *Female Genital Mutilation, also known as Female Circumcision: Information for Health Professionals* (2nd Edition). London: St Thomas' Hospital.

Moore, H. 1994. Is there a crisis in the family? *World Summit for Social Development, Occasional Paper No. 3*. Geneva: United Nations Institute for Social Development (UNRISD).

Nagel, I. 2000 *Le traffic d'Enfants en Afrique de l'Ouest, Rapport d'étude*. Osnabrück: Terre des hommes. Janvier, p. 22.

Noumbissi, A. 2003. Living conditions of the elderly in South Africa. Paper presented at the *Fourth African Population Conference*. Tunis, 8–12 December: Union for African Population Studies.

Ntozi, J.P. & Kabera, J. 1989. Marriage patterns in Ankole: South-West Uganda. *Journal of African Population Studies* No. 3. Dakar: Union for African Population Studies.

Omideyi, A.K. 1992. Family cycles and their socio-economic determinants in UAPS: *The Structure and Dynamics of Family Formation in Africa*. Dakar: Union for African Population Studies.

Oppong, C. 1982. Family structure and women's reproductive and productive roles. In R. Anker, M. Buvinic & N. Youssef (eds.), *Women's Roles and Population Trends in the Third World*. London: Croom Helm.

Oppong, C. 1991. Conjugal and parental roles in African families: old and new models. *Conference on Women, Family and Population, Vol. 1*. Dakar: Union for African Population Studies.

Oppong, C. 1992. African Family Systems in the Context of Socio-Economic Change. Paper presented at the *Third African Conference*, Dakar, Senegal, 7–10 December 1992.

Oppong, C. 1997. African family structure and socio-economic crisis. In A. Adepoju (ed.), *Family, Population and Development in Africa*. London and New Jersey: Zed Books Ltd.

Oppong, C. and Abu, K. 1987. *Seven Roles of Women: the impact of education, migration and employment on Ghanaian mothers: Women, Work and Development Series, No. 13*. Geneva: International Labour Organization.

OAU (Organization of African Unity). 1994. *Tunis Declaration on Population and Development in Africa*. Addis Ababa: Organization of African Unity.

Pearson, E. 2002. *Human Traffic, human rights: Redefining Victim Protection*. London: Anti-slavery International, p 22.

Pietila, H. 2000. Women's issues five years after Beijing: Progress and drawbacks. In *Cooperation South No. 2*. New York: UNDP.

RPG (Refugee Policy Group). 1992. *Internally Displaced Persons in Africa: Assistance Challenges and Opportunities*. Washington, DC: Refugee Policy Group.

Salah, R. 2004. Child trafficking: A challenge to child protection in Africa. Paper presented at the *Fourth African Regional Conference on Child Abuse and Neglect*. Enugu: March 2004.

Shuman, T.K. 1991. Support for the elderly: The Changing Urban Family and its Implications for the Elderly. In United Nations: *Ageing and Urbanization*. New York: United Nations.

Thahane, T.T. 1991. International labour migration in southern Africa. In D.G. Papademetrious & P. L. Martin (eds.), *The Unsettled Relationships: Labour Migration and Economic Development*. New York: Greenwood Press.

Togonu-Bickersteth, F., Akinnawo, E.O., Akinyele, O.S. & Ayeni, E. 1997. Public alms solicitation among the Yoruba elderly in Nigeria. *Southern African Journal of Gerontology*, Vol. 6, No. 2.

Unanka, G. 2002. Sharing the African experience in developing a sustainable social structure of care-giving in a society for all ages. In United Nations: *Sustainable Social Structures in a Society for all Ages*. New York: United Nations (in collaboration with HelpAge International, London).

UNAIDS. 2003. Accelerating Action against AIDS in Africa. Report presented at the *13th International Conference on AIDS and Sexually Transmitted Infections in Africa*. Nairobi, 21–26 September.

UNDP (United Nations Development Programme). 1999. *Human Development Report, 1999*. New York: Oxford University Press for UNDP.

UNECA (United Nations Economic Commission for Africa). 1992. *Dakar/Ngor Declaration on Population, Family and Sustainable Development. Report of Third African Population Conference*. Dakar, 7–12 September. Addis Ababa: UNECA.

UNFPA (United Nations Population Fund). 1999. *6 Billion: A time for choices.* New York: United Nations Population Fund.

UNFPA. 2002. *State of World Population 2002: People, poverty and possibilities.* New York: United Nations Population Fund.

United Nations. 1989. *Adolescent Reproductive Behaviour; Evidence from Developing Countries. Vol. II*. New York: United Nations.

United Nations. 1991a. *Building the smallest democracy at the heart of society.* Vienna: United Nations.

United Nations. 1991b. *1994—International Year of the Family*. New York: United Nations.

United Nations. 1998. *Population Distribution and Migration*. New York: United Nations.

United Nations. 2002a. *Africa Recovery: A troubled decade for Africa's children* (reprint). New York: United Nations Department of Public Information.

United Nations. 2002b. *Building a Society for All Ages: Second World Assembly on Ageing.* Madrid 8–12 April. New York: Department of Public Information, United Nations.

UNICEF (United Nations Children's Fund). 2000. *Child Trafficking in West Africa: Policy Responses.* Florence: UNICEF.

WSSD (World Summit for Social Development). 1995. *Declaration and Programme of Action 1995.* Copenhagen: WSSD.

Ziehl, S.C. 2004. Globalization and Family Patterns: A View from South Africa. In G. Therborn, *African Families in a Global Context. Research Report 131.* Uppsala: Nordic African Institute.

Additional bibliography

Adegboyega, O. 1992. The Structure and Dynamics of Family Formation in Africa. In *The Structure and Dynamics of Family Formation in Africa*. Dakar: Union for African Population Studies.

Adepoju, Aderanti. 1991. *Africa's Population Crisis: Formulating Effective Policies*. Africa Recovery Briefing Paper No. 3, New York: United Nations.

Adepoju, Aderanti. 2002. Situation Analysis of the Status of Women in Nigeria. *HRDC Research Series No 2*. Lagos: Concept Publications.

Adepoju, Aderanti with Mbugua W. 1993. *Rethinking Approaches to the Study of Population Dynamics in Africa*. Dakar: Union for African Population Studies.

Allen, T. & Morsink, H. (eds.). 1994. *When Refugees Go Home: African Experience*. London: James Currey Ltd.

Aryee, A.F. 1997. The African family and changing nuptiality patterns. In Adepoju, Aderanti (ed.), 1997 *Family, Population and Development in Africa*, London & New Jersey: Zed Books Ltd.

Caldwell, J.C. & Caldwell, P. 1987. The cultural context of high fertility in sub-Saharan Africa. *Population and Development Review* Vol. 13, No. 3.

Demographic Health Survey. Country reports: Zimbabwe, Zambia, Ghana, Kenya et al.

Dorkenoo, E. 1994. *Cutting the rose. Female genital mutilation: the practice and its prevention.* London: Minority Rights Publications.

Economist. 1996. A survey of the economics of ageing: All our tomorrows. *The Economist* January 27.

Evans, R. 1999. Growing old in Africa. *The Courier* No. 176, July–August. Brussels: ACP.

Hampton, J. (ed.). 1998. *Internally Displaced People: A Global Survey.* London: Earthscan Publications Ltd.

Kaseke, E. 1999. Social security and the elderly: the African experience. *The Courier* No. 176, July–August. Brussels: ACP.

Masamba, S.N. 2003. *Trafficking in Women and Children: The Situation and Some Trends in African Countries.* Kampala: UNAFRI.

Peil, M. 1995. Family help for the elderly in Africa: a comparative assessment. *Southern African Journal of Gerontology* Vol. 4, No. 2.

Toubia, N. 1995. *Female Genital Mutilation: A Call for Global Action* (2nd edition). Geneva: World Health Organization (WHO).

UNAIDS & WHO. 2003. *AIDS Epidemic Update 2003.* Geneva: United Nations.

UNFPA. 2002a. *Population, Ageing and Development; Social, Health and Gender Issues.* New York: United Nations Population Fund.

UNFPA. 2002b. *Promoting Gender Equality.* New York: United Nations Population Fund.

UNHCR (United Nations High Commission for Refugees). 2001 *Global Report 2000: Achievements and Impacts.* Geneva: UNHCR.

United Nations. 2001a. *The World Ageing Situation: Exploring a Society for All Ages.* New York: United Nations.

United Nations. 2001b. *Africa Recovery: Protecting Africa's Children—orphans, soldiers, labourers.* Vol. 15 No. 3 (October). New York: UN Department of Public Information.

World Health Organization (WHO). 2001. *Female Genital Mutilation: A Fact Sheet.* Geneva: WHO.

About the author

Professor Aderanti ADEPOJU, a Nigerian economist and demographer, was trained at the University of Ife, Nigeria and at the London School of Economics where he received his PhD in Demography in the early 1970s. He was Professor and Head of the Department of Demography and Social Statistics at the University of Ife (now Obafemi Awolowo University) in the early 1980s, and then Research Professor and Head of the Research and Advisory Services Unit, and later Dean of the Faculty of Business Administration at the University of Lagos in the late 1980s.

Adepoju has had a long and distinguished career in the international development field, working as a Regional Adviser on Population and Labour Policy for Africa for the International Labour Organization in Addis Ababa in the mid 1970s, as United Nations Chief Technical Adviser to the Government of Swaziland and the University of Swaziland in the mid 1980s, and in the decade 1988–1998 he was United Nations Population Fund's (UNFPA) Training Co-ordinator for Population, Human Resources and Development in Africa at the African Institute for Economic Development and Planning (IDEP), Dakar, Senegal. Over the past thirty years, Adepoju has assisted several African countries in capacity building, strategy development and in the development and implementation of population and development programmes. His knowledge and expertise as an economist, demographer and development specialist has been used by many of the international development organizations for which he has served as a consultant or as team leader for missions and research activities.

Adepoju has served on the Council of the Nigerian Institute of Management; the United States National Academy of Sciences, Committee on Population, and Panel on the Demography of Sub-Saharan Africa; the United Nations High Commission for Refugees External Research Advisory Committee; the Editorial Advisory Board of International Migration and International Migration Review; and as President of the Union for African Population Studies. He is a member of the Club of The Hague on Refugees and Migration; Scientific Co-ordinator of the UNESCO/Management of Social Transformation (MOST) Network of

Migration Research in Africa, and Leader of the International Organization for Migration (IOM)/UNFPA research team on emigration dynamics in sub-Saharan Africa.

Adepoju is a member of numerous international scientific associations such as the International Sociological Association, the Society for International Development, the Population Association of Nigeria, the International Union for the Scientific Study of Population, the Union for African Population Studies and others. He is currently Chief Executive of the Human Resources Development Centre based in Lagos.

Adepoju has published numerous books, monographs and scientific articles on international migration and regional integration, poverty, population and sustainable development issues, structural adjustment programmes, ageing and gender in Nigeria and Africa. A short selected list is given elsewhere in this document.

978-0-595-36464-0
0-595-36464-0